FLORAL ART

IN YOUR HOME

by Madeleine Morin

Edited by H.J.B. PIERCY

FLORAPRINT LIMITED, PARK ROAD, CALVERTON, NOTTINGHAM.   ISBN 0 903001 10 1
© EDITIONS FLORAISSE 1974, ANTONY. FRANCE.

FOREWORD

In order to preserve the essential character of the original French edition of this book most of the original illustrations have been retained in the English edition.

The sensitively worded French text has been closely translated, and then edited by Mr. Harold Piercy, Principal of the Constance Spry Flower School, to whom we are greatly indebted.

English readers will quickly realise that this book is not in the classic style of English Floral Art but will be enchanted and inspired by the beauty and inventiveness of an alternative discipline which can help to add a totally new dimension to their own arrangements.

The practical advice regarding colour, choice of plant, shape, and the many other aspects of the art, provides valuable guidance regardless of national traditions.

The Editor wishes to express gratitude to Mme. Madeleine Morin of Rheims for devoting her time and talent in creating this book.
To Countess E. von Korff, who helped enormously with her wide knowledge and practical experience in the world of flowers.
Also to M. P. Cuisance, Professor E.N.S.H. for his willing assistance in the technical research and who so competently indexed the contents of this book.

The Editor wishes also to thank Mlle. M. de Guitant, M. Harvengst (Paris) and Mlle. Madier (Rheims) for their help. He also wishes to thank M. Dumont Ets, Rheimscolour and M. Chevallier (both from Rheims), for their help with the photography.

FLORAL FASHION 1973 (Front cover)
Fashion is not long-lasting, it inspires flower decoration which marks a period with its impressive style. Fresh flowers or dry materials must be adapted to the old or modern style of decor.
The position in which the flowers will stand must be studied, and the arrangement made in correct proportion.
Flowers and all materials must be chosen in keeping with colouring and the furnishings.
The creation in the shallow dish has been arranged bearing all these points in mind.
Materials used: 3 Anthurium, 3 spider orchids, 1 white Amaryllis, 1 Allium flower head, a few branches of twisted willow forming a framework with a backing of variegated Iris leaves, all set in a pin holder.

'BOUQUET'
R. SAVERY 1612
From the Collection of the Duke of Liechtenstein

Floral art throughout the Ages and Countries

Floral decoration is not only an artistic but also an historic phenomenon. Like all historical facts, its development and decline are closely linked to the degree of civilisation and culture of each particular period.

Floral art, which was so ancient and so important to the Orientals, only took its place in the West at a relatively late date. According to Latin etymology, the 'Ars' of our ancestors signified not only an inspiration of the creative spirit, but also a manual dexterity. The 'artefix' or workman possessed this gift of transforming the raw material, thanks to his taste and his own hands.

Even if its consecration is not yet absolutely attained, it is certain, that the pleasure of making an arrangement is not a discovery of our century and that flowers have always represented a fundamental element in the everyday life of mankind. Flowers have always assumed a significant and precise role, and as a result have found their use in numerous rites and festivals.

The first examples of a floral tradition are found amongst the most ancient races practising agriculture, that is to say, several thousand years ago, in the Valley of the Nile. Many vases discovered in Egyptian tombs were destined for this use. From paintings of the times, we know that the flower most used was the lotus, which bloomed abundantly along the edge of the Nile and was the symbol of divinity.

A floral tradition just as important has left its mark on Persian, Greek and Roman civilisations. Here, flowers arranged as crowns were used for victims of holy sacrifices; there they rewarded Olympic victors or war heroes; elsewhere, strewn along the roads and hung in festoons and arches, they welcomed victorious troops. These compositions, following precise orders and laws, were undoubtedly a first outline of floral art.

Decorative foliage
Rustic calendar at
Saint-Romain-En-Gal, Rhone A.D. 200–250

(From a mosaic,
National Museum of
Roman Antiquity, Saint-Germain-en-Laye.)

Flowers also inspired poets and writers (Virgil, Homer, Sappho, to name only a few great nature lovers) which helped to extend their use and influence on customs and civilisations.

The use of flowers is not the result of pure chance. They were already cultivated with a double aim, decorative and commercial, and we know that flower growers existed who supplied florists. Flowers had their protectors, such as the King of Persia, Darius I, who in the fifth century B.C. had about fifty flower growers and florists attached to his House.

Roses, which were cultivated by the Egyptians from the fourth century B.C., were greatly appreciated in Rome. The demand for these flowers was so great that at one period it became necessary to import rose trees and to grow them in hot houses. A charming description of roses and Oleander is given by Apulee, in his Metamorphosis (Volume II, Book IV, para. II).

'. . . As I floated thus on an ocean of thoughts, I saw not far away a small valley in the shade of a thick wood; amongst all kinds of grass and rich greenery, bright scarlet roses enlivened it with their smile. And in my mind, which was not entirely that of an animal, I thought that this secret wood must be Venus and the Graces, where, amongst the thick shade, the noble flowers were resplendent in their royal brightness . . . But, as I drew near, what do I see? Not these fresh and tender roses, damp with heavenly dew and nectar, to which a blessed bramble, a fortunate thorn gave birth; and the small valley, no longer, only the bank of a brook bordered by a thick curtain of trees. These trees, of which the abundant foliage recalls that of the Oleander, bearing, like fragrant flowers, long pale red calyx, deprived of perfume; the simple countrymen called them laurel roses. If eaten, these are a deadly poison to animals . . .' (Translator: Prof. P. Vallette.)*

From drawings, literature, dried flowers found in the tombs, and recipes of essences and perfumes, we have found exactly the flower known and used at different periods. Pæonies, Irises, cornflowers, as well as poppies, lilies and violets were greatly appreciated by the Greeks and the Romans.

Between the fall of the Roman Empire and the early Middle Ages, a long period of obscurantism, poverty and regression fell upon Europe. Floral decoration, as with all other arts, was abandoned, and it is only around A.D. 1000 that it reappeared, as an item of artistic interest.

During this time, the Oriental countries, particularly China and Japan, took a very keen interest in Floral Art, which became sacred and an essential part of their way of life. A flower, according to the doctrines of Confucius, was a perfect microcosm, and as such an element of contemplation—a universe in miniature. Each flower and each plant—and these countries are rich in vegetation—represented symbolically an event in life or an intellectual and divine process. The Buddhist monks, in their profound love of nature, grew flowers to decorate their temples.

In Japan, where the art of preparing flower decoration goes back a long way, to the Masters of the Taoist philosophy, the monks had founded a flower school named Ikenobo. The Rikka, a masterpiece of floral art used in the temples at special ceremonies, was over 20 feet high and took the Master and his students several days of tireless work to complete. A Rikka is the name given to a whole scene worked with large twisted stems of a kind of Juniper Tree, symbolising rocks and plants. The Narcissus represents water in the form of a cascade. Black and red ribbons tied to the branches represent mountain peaks, and at the foot of these will be found maples, Chrysanthemums and Camellias. The gentle curve of a bare branch symbolises the moon and bathing in its light, the peak of the mountain. Below, Pæonies spread a warm glow of colour.

The Church is also responsible for the revival of floral art in Europe. It is in fact on land owned by them or in monasteries that the culture of flowers was revived. They were grown for decoration and also used to produce essences for perfume, medicinal remedies and liquors, and later were grown on a large scale for cut flower sales. Certain pagan and symbolic traditions were revived at this period, and have been handed down to us in the present day—some people still believe even now, in the power for good and evil of certain flowers.

The Crusaders also added to this renewal of interest in flowers, by bringing back from their expeditions numerous species of exotic flowers unknown in Europe.

From an old Japanese engraving representing a Rikka of the Ikenobo School in Tokyo.

It is during the Renaissance that flower arranging became an Art in Europe, following different styles, sometimes extravagant and unnatural looking, but all the more appreciated as they helped to detract from the economic and social change which menaced society at that period. This desire for floral decoration and the need to recreate nature at home is still found today, due to the same feeling of opposition to the restrictions of modern life.

The Dutch became masters in the arrangement of flowers, and many painters showed signs of this in their work during this period. A new flower appeared in Holland about 1590—the tulip; imported from the Orient by Busbecq, Ferdinand I's ambassador to the Court of Sultan Soliman II, the Magnificent. Busbecq corresponded with the famous botanist, Charles de Lecluse or Clusius (1529–1609), who was made Botany professor at Leyden in 1593. Tulips were known in England from 1572, and have since made a fortune for Holland.

During the XVIth and XVIIth centuries, floral art developed a great deal in England owing to more and more frequent contacts with the Chinese, who have always been expert gardeners and botanists. In China, flowers had already been classified in detail during the XIth century and no less than thirty-five species of Chrysanthemum had been recorded. From the very first, English flower arranging has been an individual and popular art. Towards the end of the XVIIIth century, the first books on flower arranging appeared where emphasis was laid on the combination of colour and the shape of different flowers. *(The Gardeners Dictionary,* by Phillip Miller, London, 1731–39.) Parallel with this developing interest in arranging in England, vases were manufactured to suit the particular styles of the time.

From England, the interest in floral art crossed over to America, especially Virginia, where numerous plants, unknown in Europe quickly became the joy of the English flower growers. Flower arrangements in America were made from both cultivated and wild flowers of the New World. Dried flowers for use in table decorations became the fashion, particularly for Thanksgiving Day.

In France, floral art developed a different pattern to that of Holland and England. During the Middle Ages, designs with flowers were mostly used to be reproduced in tapestries, in decoration and ornamentation of interior walls in the form of stucco work and in bas relief.

During the reign of Louis XVI, the great scenery artist, André le Nôtre specialised in garden paintings. The famous French gardens where the flower beds and paths are laid out in geometric designs were so different from those of the English style. Later the Marquise de Pompadour, a great admirer of Chinese porcelain, obtained from Louis XV large amounts of money to produce Sèvres china vases in all shapes and sizes. These were decorated with flowers and contrasted greatly with the style of Louis XIV. Everything was light and very graceful. Harmony of pastel shades was preferred to violent contrasts with often a touch of yellow being used to highlight the decoration.

Under Napoleon I, the classic designs brought over from Egypt and Italy regained importance; somewhat heavy and ornate, the decorations were of fruit and flowers grouped tightly together. Vases commemorating the victories of the Emperor were decorated with the addition of symbols, such as the Sphinx, the lion, and with bees.

In England, flower decoration acquired a new lease of life during the Victorian era, when the middle classes had more money to spend on this interest. The colouring of the decorations tended to be more subdued, due to the influence of Queen Victoria's ideas and wishes, and the shapes of the arrangements more geometric and traditional. Many books were published on the subject, and numerous classes organised. It was an essential part of one's education in those days, to know a little about horticulture and botany, and to be able to arrange flowers.

During the XXth century new artistic trends completely changed the style of flower arranging. The modern, plain and simple design in architecture and furnishings, calls for lighter rooms with brighter colours. Floral artists have again turned to the Japanese for inspiration from the Ikebana school because they feel that this style of flower arranging, emanating from the elements: Sky, Man and Earth, fits in better with the new interior designs of today. From this and other Japanese schools have developed many stylish modern flower arrangements. Changes keep taking place, and it is certain that the cycle will go round again—the Aspidistra and the Adiantum, which were so popular in the Victorian era, went out of vogue until just recently. Now they are experiencing a come-back in popularity.

*Floral decoration—Manufacturer unknown 1776.
(National Ceramics Museum, Sèvres.)*

Bouquets and flowers continue to play an essential part in our society, as they have done over the ages. Flowers are sent to welcome a new baby and to celebrate the various occasions and ceremonies during one's life: birthdays, marriage, joyful events and days of sorrow. Flowers, we hope, will always be present to show signs of affection, as a remembrance, or as a farewell gesture.

The instinctive action of a child is to offer a flower to those it loves. Every mother knows the pleasure of receiving from her child a simple bunch of flowers collected by himself. Whether the colours blend or not is immaterial in this case, since it is the thought that counts.

Florists note with interest the way lovers purchase flowers as a gift. So often they spend much time and care in choosing these, then do not like to be seen carrying them!

No official public ceremonies, either in the West or in the Orient, take place without some accompanying floral decoration. In private life and in public life, in our homes and offices, in schools, shop windows, banks and in airports, in fact everywhere we go, floral art is present.

JAMBOREE *A large festive group.*

Container: *A tall glass vase with a narrow neck. Dried and bleached grass with thin willow branches (which have been tied up at their tips after soaking) and stems of Lilium speciosum 'Jamboree'.*

A tall upright arrangement with stems all in a straight line. The delicate and fine tracery of foliage as a background, make the very beautiful lily flowers show to good advantage.

Care must be taken to see the container is always full of water, because the height of the arrangement would easily overbalance the vase.

THE MARINES 1970.

Painter: M. J. Hubert (Vresse—Belgium).

Decorator: Mme. A. Morin (Rheims).

Picture made from dry and coloured materials fixed on to a background and framed.

Reproduced $\frac{1}{10}$ of its size (approx. 6' x 3').

Flowers as with all of Nature, have always proved an inexhaustible source of inspiration to painters. Many have left behind beautiful paintings of arrangements. Some have included vases of flowers in their compositions and portraits. These paintings show a particular style of arrangement which is so attractive in shape and colours that it will never fail to please the eye of anyone who appreciates beauty. It would take too long to list here all the examples which come to mind, all the names and trends which link up painters with flowers. In passing, though, we must remember Greek vases with their elegant decorations which show a profound respect for mother nature; water-colour murals and Roman mosaics which lengthen perspective and transform walls into glorious gardens, enchanting with their rich Mediterranean flora; and again, Persian and Oriental engravings which are so graceful. Later, in the Middle Ages, flowers and foliage were used in tapestries to frame hunting scenes or groups of people and interiors of castles. Naturally the famous flower arrangements by the Flemish painters must not be forgotten. These contain so many species of flowers that it is unlikely that they could have been painted at one time, but have been added to through the flowering season. Also, remember the work of the English artists who brilliantly express their love of nature. Nearer to us, the Impressionists show in their paintings the magic of the sun and the clearness of the air, the brightness of colours and informal outlines, whilst modern painters, by the bareness of their drawings and neatness of the brush strokes, show to advantage the infinite variety of shapes which flowers give us.

We must also remember that dried flowers have now become an important item in the making of pictures and collages. By using different coloured woods and dried plant tissue, contemporary artists have created pictures with great imagination, introducing a new theme to modern art. In the pages which follow you will see a few photographs of this type of work, which show great originality and which relate to the theme of this book.

Bouquet by Flegel.
(original painting)

BOUQUET BY FLEGEL (1563–1638). *This work is the result of Luther's influence in Holland during the XVIIth century. It is a descriptive piece showing clearly the bread and wine, and has a Eucharistic theme and spiritual expression about it. The arrangement of flowers is flat fronted and without depth—each flower is standing up and faced, detached from one another, the whole group is symmetrical in shape. All the species would not be flowering together, which indicates that it was painted over a period of time, or copied from other works. The great detail on the table with the insect about to cross the bread adds to the charm of this wonderful work.*

An excellent detailed arrangement inspired by Flegel.
Arranged by Mme. Morin.

11

What is floral art?

The object of floral art is to be able to place flowers and ornamental materials, such as branches, foliage and fruits, in a harmonious fashion, the resultant collection being pleasing to the eye, suited to its surroundings, and having the ability to keep fresh and last as long as possible.

It is easy to divide floral art into two parts, one purely artistic, which is the making of the arrangement with simple and varied materials. The other, technical part, is dealing with the care and handling of the natural material, and seeing that everything remains in water in the correct positions. A flower arrangement must

MOTHER'S DAY

In a well proportioned Oriental vase, white, pale yellow and golden lilies are well arranged, expressing, symbolically, the love and affection of a child for its mother.

The undeniable grace of the flowers and choice of colours make it an arrangement that would go in any home and it would suit almost any style of furniture. The lilies used are L. regale, L. 'Golden Clarion' and L. 'Royal Gold'.

not only be lovely and in harmony with the room it decorates; it must also remain in position when moved from one place to another. It is important to support the tall stems with foliage, and to see that the vase is topped up with water when placed in its final position.

The technique of holding flowers firmly, which the professional florist understands so well, must be mastered by the amateur so that he can arrange the stems and then move them carefully without destroying the final effect. It is essential to see that whatever method one uses to hold the flowers in position, they remain firm in the container before one attempts to move it.

Amateur florists are not all artistically gifted alike. Some find it easy to understand balanced proportion, and have a good colour sense which is necessary in order to create an attractive arrangement. Others have difficulty in creating a pleasant arrangement. To the latter group, I would say that it is possible to learn the art of flower arrangement by having tuition and trying to copy good arrangements.

With experience and practice they will make interesting arrangements for themselves, even though they may still lack that special inspiration and imagination of the talented few.

The style of flower arrangements follows fashion to a certain degree. To appreciate this, compare the arrangements left to us by the renowned painters of the XVIIth century and the XVIIIth century; the prints of the 'Belle Epoque'; and the flower arrangements of today which can be admired in the shop windows of floral artists.

Like the art of drawing and painting, with which it has a great deal in common, floral art complies with the influence of the period. It evolves with time, sometimes so slowly that it is not noticed, and sometimes rapidly, when changes spring forth; such as those in the paintings of the early XXth century: Impressionism, cubism, fauvism, which have affected other forms of artistic expression. Sometimes the evolution is the result of research such as that carried out in 1965 by a group of French florists under the sponsorship of their National Trade Union which culminated in a renewal of floral art and a change of fashion. Arrangements, uniform and monotonous up to then, became more imaginative and interesting, showing signs of the oriental influence. The result was more open and less crowded arrangements, taller and with more varied flowers of good quality. With these new ideas, the other arrangements appeared old fashioned. More recently a new tendency for less tall arrangements has become the vogue, using a more horizontal line with masses of larger flowers.

A STUDY IN OUTLINES

The flowers are carefully placed in line in a narrow, upright, modern glass vase. This gives an overall sensation of elongation. No foliage is added to break this line, but three buds of Ranunculus and a stem of ivy— variety 'Conglomerata', soften the stiffness of the roses and Iris.

The roses and Irises have had all their foliage removed and the stems have been cleared of surplus material so that they fit into the small opening in the glass vase. The stems remain visible to help balance the arrangement. Three Anemones add depth of colour and weight to the base of the vase. The vase and its contents reflected in the table top are in perfect colour harmony.

FLOWER DECORATED HARNESS

In early May, when lilac is at its best, it is fun to use it in a novel way. Here we have a saddle set up on a wrought iron stand which has been decorated with tree pæony foliage, a few of the heavenly flowers, and a profusion of perfumed white and mauve lilac flower heads. Much of the lilac foliage has been removed. All the flower stems are arranged into blocks of soaked oasis, carefully covered with wire netting and hidden by short pieces of foliage.

It is a recognised fact that fresh flowers always contrast well against the shiny surface of well polished leather goods, such as books in a bookcase.

As soon as they are cut, place the flowers flat on a ground sheet or into a flat basket named a 'cueillette' (flower gathering). (I always prefer to cut straight into a bucket of warm water.) If using a sheet, place the heaviest blossoms underneath and the more delicate on top, in order not to bruise and damage them; carry them to a cool, dark place and start preparing them straight away. Remove all foliage that will not be needed. Have plenty of deep containers with fresh water ready to hold the flowers and foliage. Flowers with weak stems must be rolled up in stiff paper to help straighten them whilst they are having a long drink. Once fully turgid, they should remain straight, or at least develop interesting curves without flopping over, e.g. tulips. The flowers should be left in these conditions for several hours before attempting to arrange them. By doing so, they will last much longer when taken into the house. In towns, where people have no gardens, flowers can be bought from shops and flower sellers. These should be carefully studied and only bought from reputable firms if one is to expect them to last a long time.

Foliages and fruit can be made good use of in some arrangements. Some such as Caladium, Croton and Strelitzia, from hot houses, are very fine for exotic groups. The foliage and berries of such things as Cotoneaster, Rhus cotinus and Symphoricarpus, have very decorative properties and an advantage over the more delicate plants in that they last well in water.

Wild flowers should not be forgotten. Reeds, leaves, berries and fruits collected from the hedgerows whilst on a country walk, make very pretty and long-lasting arrangements. Amongst the most useful are the thistle, bullrush, wild grasses and wild clematis, and these will all dry well. Today one finds these added to exotic dry materials from abroad which are available from most flower shops in the autumn. When carefully arranged and in the correct positions they make very good decorations.

Harmony of colours and shapes

The colour of flowers, which is never ending, is one of their main attractions. When colours are mixed in a decoration they must be cleverly used to get the best effect. Some colours go well together while others do not. Although there are really no rules and it is a matter of taste, here are a few guiding lines to help with obtaining successful arrangements: Three fundamental colours exist: blue, yellow and red, with many other colours being formed between these, notably orange, green and violet. Depending on whether the colours of the petals radiate or absorb the light rays, so one gets lighter or darker shades of colour. White is the result of total reflection of incidental light, the very dark or blackish shades, that of almost complete absorption. Generally the use of two fundamental colours is pleasant; blue and yellow, red and yellow, for example. It is the same when using one main colour with a secondary colour close by e.g. red and green. Although this needs care, blue and orange, which is correct, is not everybody's choice when used in flower decoration. With tints of these two colours the effect can be very different. Monochrome arrangements, or those made from flowers of different tints of the same colour can be very pleasing to the eye. A vase of the following coloured Delphiniums: violet, lilac, mauve, amethyst, lavender blue, sky blue and pale blue; can be very beautiful together. Harmonising equally well are the sulphur yellow, buttercup yellow, saffron, and yellow-orange of the Indian rose.

Bleached and natural dried materials are generally of neutral colours: greys, beiges, light and dark browns and blackish colours, and blend well together. Those which are artificially coloured seem to be very popular at present and add an interesting touch of brightness to austere or sombre arrangements, but they must not be discordant. Some people will not have dyed flowers at any price.

Purple, red or wine coloured flowers placed next to orange or vermilion do not go well—this is due to the luminous brightness of the orangey shades making the red colours dull.

REALITY

This pleasant arrangement stands for freshness and peace. In a shallow flat dish, the flowers look well, rising amongst moss and pebbles.

It is simple to arrange; the Iris flowers and Equisetum (that terrible weed of badly drained areas) are held in position by pin holders. The flower stems are of different lengths and the stiffness has been taken away by the softer line of the Equisetum and Iris leaves. The moss will do well in the moisture of the shallow dish.

Very dark coloured flowers must be used with care as in a mixed arrangement they do not show up and from a distance the group seems to have gaps in it which look unsightly. White flowers on the other hand highlight a group. It will be noted that a little white in mixed arrangements shows up the other tints. Sometimes pink and red are not good together unless a wide range of each colour is used, and the vase has the correct background. Whites and yellows always go together well. As I have already mentioned, colour in flower arranging is a matter of personal taste. Before starting the arrangement, it is good to place all the materials together just to see what the final effect will be. Perhaps the addition of a few white flowers or some silver foliage will tie it all up together and complete an excellent picture.

Do not forget that the vase or container must be considered in the over-all picture. What has been said about the flowers also applies to the vase in which they will be placed. They must harmonise with each other. Sometimes flowers are arranged without foliage, but in most cases they have their own leaves, or leaves of other plants added to the group. These leaves cover a wide range of greens, yellow-greens or dark greens, together with other colours of purple, golden-yellow shades, blue-greens and silver-greys; and in the autumn, foliages acquire wonderful colours too numerous to list here. Fruits are just as varied, adding yellows, lime greens, oranges and reds, and with berries, more colours of blue, violet and whites. One can see a great variety of fruits and berries on garden shrubs such as Cotoneaster, holly, Symphoricarpus, Callicarpa, etc.

PASTEL

An unusual design made from a group of pink and blue Delphiniums, together with 3 Eremurus seed heads, 5 garlic seed heads and one piece of Stachys lanata. All the colours are pale green and pastel shades. The graceful, slender stems are supported at their base by the large round garlic inflorescences.

This modern group is built up in 3 tiers, with blocks of oasis, backed by a high upright sheet of copper. This is securely fixed to the base which is hidden by the garlic seed heads. The flowers of harmonising colours are arranged at appropriate levels to give a slender shape, and the whole structure hidden by the Delphinium foliage.

They are very ornamental and last a long time. The shapes of the flowers are as varied as their colours; besides rounded and large flowers carrying a single stem e.g. exhibition Dahlia, are small or medium sized flowers. Some are on single stems, others are carried with many on a compound stem or grouped in elongated inflorescences of a completely different character. The former give a solidarity to the arrangement, the latter, grace and elegance. Some flowers, however large, appear light in an arrangement and give it special interest. 'Peace' roses, cactus Dahlias and long spurred columbines come to mind. These different shaped flowers can be mixed in an arrangement and bring harmony and balance to the whole group. It is the positioning of the flowers that is important and often, (but not always, as can be seen in the Dutch paintings already mentioned) the large flowers are better placed near the centre of the arrangement, the lighter flowers and buds being used in the outline. Arrangements can also be made up with all one type of flower e.g. different Chrysanthemums. When collecting flowers and foliage to make a decoration, consideration should be given to the materials used. Such as lasting qualities of each, the texture of foliage and flowers, and contrast of materials. All these points play an important part in the overall finished picture.

ANCIENT BASKETWORK

Set against a background of a rich XVIIth century tapestry, this old-fashioned two-tier basket filled with bright coloured flowers is very eye catching.

To arrive at the required size, the whole arrangement has been set on a wooden base and the extra height is obtained from a vertical, gnarled branch.

Both trays of the container are filled with wet oasis covered with wire netting which will help secure and support the flowers, at the same time allowing them plenty of moisture. I would suggest that the top flowers are in tubes.

This particular arrangement is of pale yellow Irises, Rose 'Mme A. Meilland', white tulips, blue cornflowers, guelder roses, lily of the valley and a few Ixia. The colours chosen tie up with the flower filled baskets appearing in the tapestry in the background.

Decoration styles

All the arrangements in this book belong to the contemporary Western style. As has already been said, for the past ten years, this has been influenced by the Oriental style in which there are fewer flowers but greater importance is given to their shape and placing, rather than to the colour and amount of flowers used in the decoration.

This book does not deal with Oriental art packed with symbolism, and which requires serious study by those concerned. The Japanese style would require a book on its own; only the enlightened can understand its subtle meaning. We have, however, a few compositions showing its influence without falling under its rules.

It goes without saying that the contemporary style of flower arranging is the most practised at present, but it is not the only style that the flower arranger can employ. It is sometimes necessary to adapt the style of decoration to the type of furniture or style of the room. Evidently, it is through the painters that we know the trends of floral art through the centuries. However, it is also possible through reading historical records to form the following conclusions: The homes of the XVIth and XVIIth centuries were decorated with many and varied flowers, placed in finely worked vases. This kind of décor brings to mind stately life at court, in particular those of Louis XIV, which shows itself up so well in the 'French Gardens'. In the XVIIIth century, flower decorations, although still large and full of beautiful things, became more refined, lighter and elegant. The vases in which they were arranged being more artistic in shape. The Anglo-Saxon influence appeared under the reign of Louis XVI which brought more natural flower arrangements. The rapid evolution of art in all its aspects expressed itself in the following period by taller arrangements and the use of many more flowers than at the present time—the Empire style is characteristic of this. During the XIXth century both asymmetrical arrangements and symmetrical arrangements appeared together along with the use of mixed tropical fruits with flowers—some brought back to England from the colonies. It is from there that flower arranging progressively developed towards present-day shapes, bearing the influence of fashion, professional research and that of Oriental art. At present a great deal of imagination goes into the use of many varied materials in flower decoration. It is difficult to define contemporary floral art precisely. The introduction of many vegetable species from America since the XVIth century, and the Far East in the following period, the hybridisations of plants and plant breeding which have brought forth magnificent varieties, have given florists materials of greater value which their predecessors did not have available.

A number of these materials, however, were used in the older days, and perhaps some of the old-fashioned flowers were more beautiful than those today. One could not fault the presence of tulips or Chrysanthemums in the Renaissance decorations introduced only at the end of the XVIIIth century in decorations of Louis XIV style. The important thing in flower decoration is that it should fit in with the style of the room. The choice of the flowers and the vase should correspond with the furnishings and the colour of the carpet and curtains. Here again the use of colour harmony crops up which has been mentioned already. Against a dark background, light flowers will show up best, particularly those of warm colourings: yellows, oranges, vermillion, coral pink or cream. Against a light background, a dark group will produce the maximum effect.

It is important not to make a flower arrangement before knowing the position in which it is to be displayed. A beautiful arrangement can look completely wrong in a setting for which it has not been designed. The flowers, container and surroundings form a trio which cannot be separated.

HARVEST FESTIVAL

A glorious splash of autumnal colour is displayed in this antique copper basket.
Two pieces of twisted root have cleverly been fixed to make a background on which fruits and
flowers have been carefully arranged. The many sizes and colours of Dahlia give a rich feel to the
group. The Sorbus foliage and fruits blend well with the small grape tomato trusses
and the Pyracantha.
A pleasing arrangement, excellently displayed against an ideal background.

Line and colours

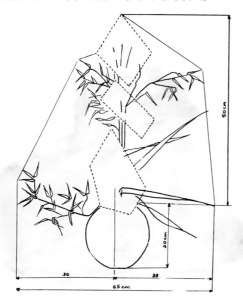

Bamboo and Gladioli leaves form the shape of the arrangement which is predominantly green. The copper and yellow single Chrysanthemums give a touch of colour at three levels down the centre of the vase. Materials needed to copy this arrangement: An 8″ round, flat-based, modern blue-green glass bowl, which sits firmly on its 3″ wide base. The coloured glass blends well with the green of the Bamboo and Gladioli foliage.

The 3 Bamboo stems and 4 Gladioli leaves are secured firmly, then the Chrysanthemums placed separately. Fix the height first with the yellow single spray, then in the middle area place the copper coloured spray. Then fill in the base with the mixed yellow and copper flowers, plus the bud which is important.

This could be arranged in wire netting or oasis and should last well because the stems should have plenty of water in the type of vase shown here.

Principles of flower decoration

The success of a flower arrangement lies mainly in the proportion kept between its height and its width, and the proportion between the arrangement itself and the container.

As a rule, flower arrangements can be contained in an imaginary geometric shape, a sphere, a spherical section, a cylinder, a cone or a pyramid, etc. giving a rounded, rectangular, square or triangular line. The proportions to be observed between the various shapes are important. In a slender triangular arrangement it is possible that the flowers may reach twice, to two and a half times the height of the container. This will depend entirely on the materials used and its visual appearance. There should be no strict rules. Care must be taken not to exaggerate the height to the extent of making the vase look top-heavy. As to its width, it can vary between two-thirds and four-fifths of its height. A vase 8″ high can contain an arrangement 20″ high and from 12″–16″ wide.

With a little experience, it will not be necessary to make measurements, and proportion and balance will come naturally. For beginners, it is a help to keep to dimensions as a guide to save making serious mistakes. Professionals in flower arranging can very cleverly arrange flowers to suit any size of container. Beginners will find it easier to start with a bunch of flowers and choose a vase to hold the flowers afterwards. There is a great art in arriving at the right material to suit the vase. It must be remembered whatever the value or the beauty of the vase, the overall effect is the important factor and the flowers must be in keeping, and are an essential part of the arrangement.

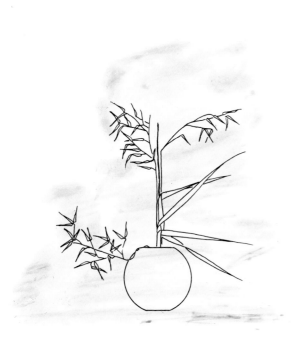

Arrangement: this is roughly contained with a triangle 26" at the base and 20" in height. The Gladioli leaves point in two directions—the bamboo balance on the left and in the top of the triangle. The Chrysanthemums are placed either side of the main axis, forming the topmost point of 28". This arrangement has been secured to a supporting rod between the pieces of bamboo. The Gladioli leaves, grouped to the right and the lower part of the arrangement are placed one by one and diagonally bent to form the necessary shape.

The copper and yellow flowers rise vertically and give a touch of colour, yellow predominating. Use shorter flowers to tuck in at the bottom of the vase.

Flower arrangements can be symmetrical or asymmetrical. The former were popular in the past and still make lovely arrangements today, but the asymmetrical shapes are the ones more usually seen. The triangular outline of an arrangement is normally less symmetrical with a spray of flowers on one side, not necessarily balanced with one on the other side. This does not appear incorrect if the arrangement is visually well balanced by other flowers nearer the centre of gravity at the vase base. The asymmetrical shapes can be accentuated even more to an L or an S. Symmetry is not necessary in flower decorations if the flowers are sufficiently well balanced.

This only comes after much practice with placing flowers in the vase and then studying the effect from a distance. Experience counts in this type of arrangement, especially when doing a pair of vases when one has to curve from left to right and the other vice-versa.

In all flower arrangements an imaginary main line must be distinguished around which the group is built and forming at the same time, the structure. Beginners tend to place each flower separately and in opposite directions. It is better to fix the outline first, all stems flowing into a centre point. Stems of different lengths should be used, and any curved stems placed in the correct flowing lines. As the arrangement develops, support the outline by shorter stems going in the same direction—no two flowers of the same length should be together.

Some people find it easier to fill in sections then join these up with the last few flowers or foliage. Care should be taken to see that the flowers and foliage look natural as if they still belong to the plant, many flowers have a face which must be taken into account. It is very important to get all stems flowing from a centre point. If these elementary rules are not followed, the arrangement will never look correct.

When floral arrangements are seen from one side only, or as an all-round group, it is important to see that they have depth to the material and this is obtained by having the flowers placed at

The study of curves

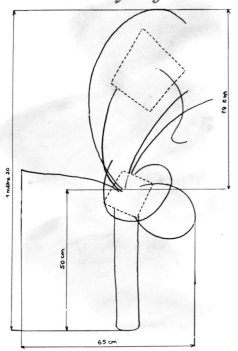

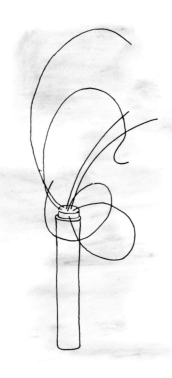

An arrangement in a narrow Madoura cylindrical vase from Vallauris. Curved spiral stalks entwine Lilium auratum supported by stems of Pyracantha.

To complete this arrangement take a 20" x 5" cylinder vase in a varnished orange and shaded black colourings. If there is any doubt about balance, half fill it with damp sand to add weight to the base. For the outline, 6 natural curving stems of Desmodium, 2 branches of berried Pyracantha and a branch of birch.

three or four different levels and in different planes; again all stems flowing from a centre point.

In this work, care must be taken to avoid symmetry and the emphasis is on balance. Follow the natural line of the stalks and reeds, which are anything from rigid and straight, to supple and distorted. Make use of all these factors. Rigid lines are neat but lack grace and elegance which supple, curved and distorted lines possess.

Distortion can bring a touch of oddness and peculiarity, which is called for in some modern arrangements.

Another important question is the placement of flowers. Should flowers and foliage be used closely packed together, or on the contrary be spaced, to give lightness? This is a difficult answer to give because so much depends on the type and style of the decoration. No arrangement should be so massed that the flowers do not

show properly, and a good guide to follow for everyday decorations is: if in doubt, leave out. So many arrangements are overcrowded.

During summer and autumn, many flowers are available and usually cheaper to purchase, when they can be used in a mass of colour. This gives a good splash of colour in a room. A profusion of flowers may be necessary to copy certain styles of flower arranging, however, arrangements made with a limited number of choice flowers also have their charm and are more suited to our time. A simple bleached or whitened root forming a container with a few interesting or rare flowers and two or three lovely leaves worked into it will make a distinctive decoration. Of course it is more difficult to compose this type of decoration than those containing many flowers. The positioning of the few flowers is of great importance and makes all the difference to the arrangement—one ill-placed flower will stand out a mile. We rely on this type of arrangement when flowers are in

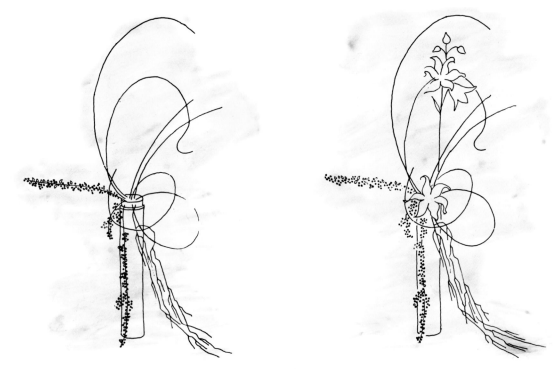

The only flowers are 1 stem and 1 single bloom of Lilium auratum.

To make the arrangement, take the natural curving branches and place carefully in the moistened oasis. Next, place the two pieces of Pyracantha on the left hand side, balancing this with the birch branch on the right. Finally place the complete stem of Lilium auratum into position with the single flower at the base, linking flowers and foliage to the vase.

short supply and expensive. It is not always the amount of flowers in the arrangement that makes it beautiful—it is the way in which they are used that makes the overall effect. The spaces between each flower often enhance their value and give at the same time elegance to the composition. It is with this in mind that branches are carefully thinned down and stems are denuded of superfluous foliage, when a lighter effect would be advantageous. Not only will it help flowering shrubs to last longer, but the value of the flowers will be doubled e.g. Philadelphus.

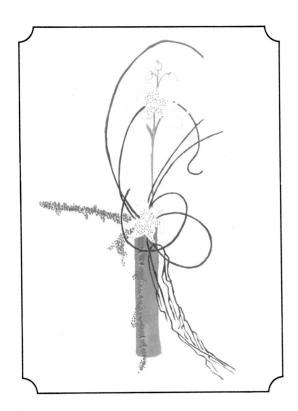

A winter decoration

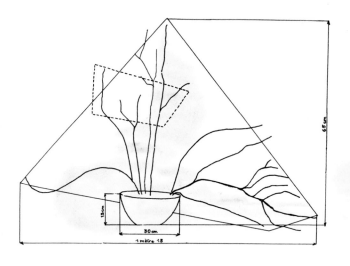

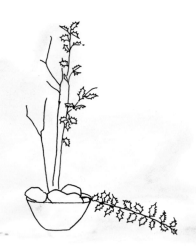

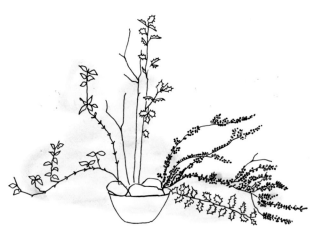

Materials: A Madoura pottery bowl from Vallauris.

Large pieces of stone for base of vase and smaller stones of various shapes and sizes to go on top. 2 stems of Forsythia, 2 branches of Dictamnus (burning bush), 1 stem of holly with berries, 2 stems of plain green holly, 2 branches of Japanese quince, 3 Christmas roses and a small branch of purple Mahonia.

To make the arrangement, place the branches carefully between the stones, first the quince, in an upright position, with the green holly next to it. Then fit in the burning bush with the holly berries coming out over the front. The Christmas roses are carefully placed at the base of the vase with the Mahonia. I would suggest that a pinholder placed first at the base and then the stones around this, would give a much more secure finish to the arrangement.

ANEMONES

A bunch of about twenty stems of Anemones is enough to fill a small vase. They will last well and take up flowing lines as they develop. Although none of their own foliage is supplied with them, the green calyx gives a charm to the arrangement.

Anemones are particularly suited for small table arrangements, being normally short stemmed. Or to brighten up an area close to photographs in a sitting room. They look very attractive arranged in a shallow wicker basket.

To make this arrangement, line the basket with polythene or oiled paper, and then stand a shallow glass dish containing wire netting in the bottom of it. Pack round with damp moss. One could fill the basket with moss and then pack the stems into this, but it would not be so long lasting as when the stems are actually in water. Add a little heather and Mahonia leaves to get another shape to the arrangement. Group the colours and arrange the Anemones around at different heights to avoid a flat solid look. This arrangement can be done in oasis but it is not easy to get Anemones firmly fixed in this. They will last a long time if well looked after.

How to arrange flowers

OPULENCE

Here we have a high cone made up of a variety of flowers, standing in an antique white flower-pot cover. It is a good example of a luxurious decoration for a big room. Used for a special occasion only because it would be costly to produce. The photograph shows a cone of excellent proportions, testifying the masterly technique and artistic touch of the author. Notice the use of different types of flower and the position of the darker colours to the centre, to give weight and balance. The cone consists of lilies in orange, yellow and white, Alstræmeria, snapdragons, Ornithogalum and Chrysanthemums.

The container holds a special iron structure with 3 tiers, each packed with oasis into which the flowers are fixed. A wire netting cone can be made and stuffed with damp moss, and again flowers can be pushed into this, but they would only last for a short period. The oasis is much more expensive to use, but the flowers would last for a longer period.

After the vase and flowers of different shapes and colours have been chosen, all that remains is to fix them in the correct place to make the picture which has already been conjured up in the mind. Several rules must be observed however. First the overall size must be worked out to get the correct proportions. Do not overfill the vase with water—top up when the arrangement is completed and resting in its final position.

No foliage should remain on the stalks which go below the water line, these take up room and soon make the water smell. With heavily foliated materials, thin out a little to check transpiration, and if necessary, add a few stems of only foliage to fill in later. Generally the main stems forming the height are first placed in the vase, then those at the sides, followed by those at the front—to give depth to the arrangement. One or two stems coming in from the back to the centre, help to give fullness in certain groups. Now fill in the remaining spaces, keeping the larger flowers towards the centre. If any appearance of lightness is required, it will not be necessary to add extra foliage. If a heavier effect is required, then a few leaves will help.

The flower stems should flow from a central point—it may be to one side of the vase in certain arrangements, but no stems should cross one another. See that each stem is in the correct position and each flower shows up well. In old paintings of flower arrangements there are often many flowers used but each one is well positioned and never hides another. Never use more flowers or foliage than is necessary.

The arrangement must be firm when finished—this is only arrived at if the container is properly wired up at the start. Any accessories such as candles should be held with floral tape, glue or other fixing aids. Stones and pebbles help to add weight, especially when using shallow containers.

Ribbons, fruits and fir cones must be carefully wired before placing in the vase. This is done by threading a wire through each item and securing it to the short stem or ribbon, to make a false stem which can then go into the group. Once completed, carefully study the arrangement from all angles to see if it can be improved in any way.

SIMPLICITY IN WHITE AND BLUE

No manual skill is required to place the two twisted stems of flowering Stephanotis into this delicate, blue Japanese vase. The resulting effect of this simple decoration is very pleasing, the beauty of both the Stephanotis and the vase going so well together.

A little advice

Leafy stems, flowering stems, berries and fruit are living materials. All the time there is a movement of moisture in their cells and a change of gases going on, in the main through the leaf surface. Only when this process exists does the plant remain in good condition. Once the plant material is cut from the parent plant, the intake of moisture is checked. Even when in water it does not work in quite such an effective way. To reduce transpiration and help keep the cut stems looking fresh, it may help to remove some of the leaves, especially in winter time when room temperatures are often very high and the atmosphere very dry. Some people recommend removing all leaves from the flowering stems and adding shorter leafy stems to the vase to help make the flowers last longer.

Cut stems absorb water. When picking flowers get them into water as soon as possible and before the base of the stem seals up naturally. If flowers are bought from a market, often this sealing will have taken place, so cut them straight away upon reaching home. Some people recommend cutting stems under water—this prevents bubbles of air forming in the capillary tubes, which sometimes causes an air lock. It may help to split the stem or, with woody stems, to crush the bottom $\frac{1}{2}$" to break up the fibres. When stems or branches have a thick bark to them, this should be peeled off about an inch up the stem. All stems should be cut at an angle, giving a wider absorbing area and also stopping the chance of an air lock when the stems touch the base of the container. If flowers still seem to flag after all these different treatments, wrap the whole stems in stiff paper and immerse the tips in really hot water for about thirty seconds; then place the whole bundle in warm, deep water for a few hours. By rolling up the bundle in stiff paper, the stems will be held straight and will remain so when the cells become turgid again. Soft tissue and newspaper are useless because they will not hold the stems firmly. If the flower heads go over and are not wrapped up before being treated, often they are too heavy to return to the upright position.

With certain plants, such as all the Euphorbia family, Poinsettia and poppies; the cut stem secretes a creamy fluid which must be checked. This can be done by sealing in a flame or dipping the tip of the cut surface into boiling water for a few seconds. Some people treat Gerbera in the same way to help them last in water.

The large and coloured anthers of many lilies are very decorative but unfortunately the pollen they carry will badly stain any fabric on which they may fall. Remove these anthers very carefully by lifting off the filament with tweezers or with your thumb and first finger. Never cut them off because this will result in bruising the filament tissue. Flowers with the anthers removed are said to last a little longer.

Thorns should be removed from rose stems carefully, by rubbing off with finger and thumb, or the back of one's scissors—this helps with water absorption and saves damaging foliage when wrapping them up. They are, of course, easier to carry without thorns. Carnations should always have their stems cut between the nodes. The first two flowers can be removed from the tip of Gladioli which seems to help the rest of the flowers to develop. Violets drink through their petals and benefit from being immersed in water from time to time.

Generally, amateur arrangements are built without artifice and look natural, the use of wire, if not totally excluded, should only be used in exceptional cases and be very discreet. Wiring of flowers should only be done in true bouquet work—it will give extra support which is necessary and also makes possible certain shaping which otherwise could not be carried out. Zinnia have a habit of bending over at the neck which is so often a very weak place and wiring is permissible in this case—done internally through the flower heads down into the stem. Some florists wire all their flower arrangements, but this should be discouraged.

It is possible to bend a stem slightly by carefully pulling it through one's fingers, slowly and under a little pressure, until the desired shape is obtained. This cannot be hurried and requires a little skill—a false move and the stem will snap. Sometimes the base of thick stems, e.g. Arum lilies and Amaryllis, split at the base and the stem tissue curls upwards making it difficult to place the stems into netting. To stop this curling, place a rubber band or a piece of raffia tightly round the stem base.

It may be necessary to extend stems to get the required height for some arrangements. This can be done by firmly fixing a number of small containers or tubes to sticks which are then worked into the vase. These are filled as separate units and worked into the foliage in such a way as to appear as one large group. By doing this,

A LARGE COLOURFUL ARRANGEMENT

A few burning logs in the hearth and the last of the autumn flowers bring colour to this rather dark room.

Standing on a dark polished table is an antique white pottery flowerpot holder full of many different flowers in autumnal colourings, giving the idea of the Dutch painters in the XVIIth century. The colours of violet, deep reds, pinks, mauves, bright yellows and bronze can be found in this group. The flowers include: Cosmos, Cactus and pompon Dahlia, Helichrysum, Rudbeckia, Michaelmas Daisy, Helianthus and Echinops. Amaranthus hangs down on the right-hand side like ribbons, and at the base of the container are fruits of Alsatian plum, apple and a head of decorative Kale.

PERSIAN RANUNCULUS

To make this arrangement, which is somewhat different from the classical style, a very modern, heavy vase in slate-blue and pink ceramic has been chosen. It is first filled with oasis and then pieces of dried wood are securely fixed to the centre through which the brown cord is threaded which dominates the picture with its loops, twists and curled ends. Groups of pink Ranunculus of varying shades form the basis of the arrangement and emphasize the pink colour in the container.

TULIPS IN PROFUSION

Wicker baskets in all forms are always popular. In the picture you will see that an open-work, straight-sided, bucket-type basket with a handle has been chosen to hold tulips. The wide opening in this type of container makes for straightforward arranging, and many stems can easily flow into it. During May a selection of tulips from the open ground is available, such as Darwin, Parrot, Cottage and Breeder types, which provide a broad range of colours. Their long and rigid stems lend themselves to the upright group yet, at the same time, are used to create flowing lines at the sides.

To make this arrangement, fix a bowl or deep metal lining to the basket and then add 2" wire netting through which the tulip stems are threaded. This may be covered later by adding moss to the surface, or tucking down some short-growing flowers as in the picture. Baskets often have a rough base, so should be stood on a mat or piece of felt to protect the surface of your furniture.

special short flowers, such as lily of the valley, can be worked into a group of large flowers. They must, of course, be put in clusters rather than in individual stems, to show them up. Normally these are only used in really large decorations where it would be impossible to get stems of the required length.

From time to time it is necessary to use special equipment in a vase to hold flowers in position. For example, tie a bunch of leaves together to help hold stems in place, or introduce a small piece of wire netting through which the stems are threaded—this will help a great deal in flower tubes. In a transparent vase of glass or crystal, the netting must be kept just around the rim, which can then be hidden by leaves and by the flowers themselves. Moss is also used to hide the mechanics in a shallow container. A few well-placed natural stems can look attractive through glass and add to the arrangement, but a mass of muddled stems, oasis or florapack, certainly do not and should be hidden at all costs.

It is not a good idea to colour the water or try to line the inside of the vase with foliage to try to hide the stems.

Plenty of ordinary domestic tap water is the best for flowers. In vases the water must be maintained at the correct level by constantly adding to it—at least once a day. It is better not to keep changing it, but to start with a clean container, wire netting and stems free from leaves, and whilst it keeps clear, just adding water. A few drops of a disinfectant will help to check the build-up of bacteria in the water. Aspirin or a trace of copper will have the same effect. The action of sugar is debatable. Certain commercial chemicals certainly do help, but add to the cost of the arrangement.

The position in which flowers are placed in the room is of major importance, and draughts, high temperatures from radiators and smoke-filled rooms should be avoided whenever possible. A steady, even temperature is best, about 55°F; rather than having them in heat during the day and then placing them in the cool at night.

FLOWERS AND SCULPTURE

This piece of sculpture is one of many in Rheims Cathedral, and depicts a 'cripple' who seems over-burdened with the weight of her infirmity.
On this occasion the weight is made up from the flower arrangement. The beautiful materials are arranged in a hidden shallow container and consist of deep blue Iris, orange Gerbera, yellow lilies, snapdragon and Gerbera, white lilies and snapdragons, and in the centre, a group of variegated ivy, which blend so well with the stone background. A simple group of the same materials arranged in a small stone plinth, balances the setting.

Equipment

An amateur florist or flower arranger will need a certain amount of equipment to carry out her work with flowers. The equipment should consist of the following:

A good, strong pair of scissors or secateurs, which will cut well and not tear the stem tissue. Preferably with one cutting blade, which may be sharpened, and a good, hard cutting plate.
A sharp penknife is useful to some people but a hazard to others—good for rose thorns.
Flower scissors which will cut all thin stems, wire netting and the odd florists wire.
Wires of different thickness for supporting and wiring flowers, fruits, etc.
Fresh moss, in which to arrange flowers.
Oasis, florapack and styrofoam, for all types of arrangements.
Oiled paper in which to place damp moss.
Pinholders and oasis holders.
Adhesive wax to hold candles, etc.
Materials for tying—raffia, oasis tape, gutta-percha tape.
Stones, pebbles, fine gravel, glass marbles and broken windscreen glass, to add to shallow containers as a point of interest, and to hide holding devices e.g. pinholders.
A flower spray—pressurised, to give a fine mist.
A small watering can with a long spout.

The most useful item is the flower scissors, which should always be kept clean, well oiled and sharp.

Flowers will not always stay in the position in which they were placed, particularly when the vase has a very wide top to it. Wire netting will help to hold the flowers in position. It should be placed in the container so that it touches the bottom and forms a network of strands right to the top of the container. For tall arrangements it should go above the rim for support. Roll the netting into an evenly distributed bundle and press it into the vase, sharp ends should be turned inwards. Silver and fragile vases should be first lined with paper, or plastic covered netting should be used, to avoid scratching. Try placing thin canes through the tangle of 2″ mesh netting to see that it is not too compact, before using fresh flowers in it. Too much netting is worse than having no netting at all. Secure netting by bending over the vase edge or by tying it in like a parcel.

If wired flowers are used in the arrangement, beautiful and original shapes may be obtained by bending them carefully. (Very much frowned upon in certain circles and not allowed in competitive work.)

Pinholders with heavy bases exist in various sizes and with different pins.

If heavy branches are to be used, it may be necessary to fix the pinholder with plasticine or place a heavy stone or glass around it to hold it firmly down. Plastic pinholders are quite hopeless.

Oasis will often be mentioned in this book. It is a water-retaining substance which holds stems very firmly in position. It acts as a sponge and holds a large amount of water which keeps most flowers fresh. It can be used in its own dry state for dry materials. It cannot be used for many times, because every time a stem goes into the 'sponge' it makes a hole which remains and eventually crumbles. For added support use in conjunction with wire netting.

Oasis is usually purchased in blocks which can then be cut to different sizes according to requirements. It can also be bought as balls, cylinders and cones, but these are naturally more expensive in the long run.

Florapack does not have the same qualities as oasis and cannot be used in quite the same way. It has to be broken up to absorb water and then packed into the container. It can be used over and over again, and some flowers last longer in it than in oasis, e.g. roses and lily of the valley.

The four-prong oasis holders—as illustrated at the top of page 38 have an adhesive base to them which, when pressed down into the container, will hold quite firmly. It is important to see that the surface is completely dry before attempting

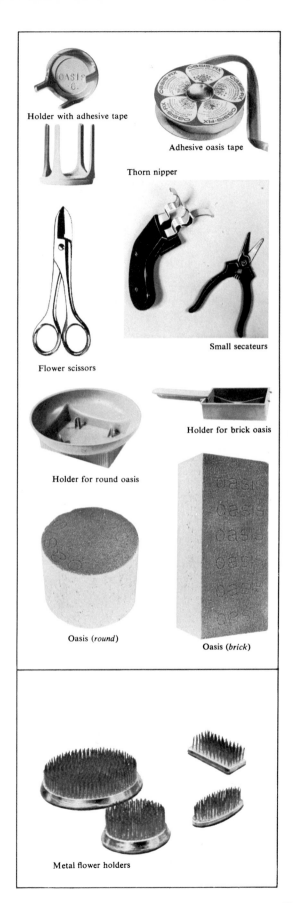

Holder with adhesive tape

Adhesive oasis tape

Thorn nipper

Flower scissors

Small secateurs

Holder for round oasis

Holder for brick oasis

Oasis (*round*)

Oasis (*brick*)

Metal flower holders

to fix the holder, because it will not stick to a damp or greasy surface. Once secure, the wet oasis on top will not affect its holding capacity.

Gutta-percha, and many other flower tapes are of a rubbery nature and grip as they are slightly stretched whilst binding stems and wire surfaces. They help support flower stems and prevent wires rusting and at the same time, they colour the false stems to match in with the bouquet. Available in natural, white, greens and browns usually, but some American tapes do cover a much wider range of colours.

THE RISING SUN

The bright red flowers are carefully arranged in a 'Murano Bamboo' glass vase which has marbles at its base to weight it down. At the rim of the vase a piece of cork bark or Canna rhizome is securely fixed, through which the flower stems are threaded.

A tall stem of Ficus benjamina is first set in position to give the shape to the arrangement. It has had a few leaves removed to give a light, elegant effect. Tulips rise up into the centre spray of foliage and another 3 branches go to the left—again denuded of their leaves. The weight of 3 stems of Amaryllis on the right and down to the centre point balance the arrangement. The Amaryllis leaves add interest at the base and help follow the very distinct flow of the arrangement. A very good colour scheme against the background.

A wide selection of basket work

1

2

3

4

5

6

7

8

9

10

11

A WELCOMING ARRANGEMENT

The horizontal structure and surprising proportions give this arrangement a strange and unusually light effect which is not easy to obtain with a narrow necked vase. Made up from long slender stems with seed pods (Spanish broom), alder cones and a stem of cedar in the centre to right hand side. The centre flowers are those of Gaillardia and the spray on the right-hand side a stem of spider orchids. The narrow-necked vase and silver-grey background display this arrangement to good advantage.

WICKERWORK

No 1   High handled, round basket on a foot.
No 2   Boat-shaped basket with high, oval handle.
No 3   Posy basket.
No 4   Large open work oval basket.
No 5   Oblong picking basket.
No 6   Picking basket.
No 7   High-backed display basket for fruit.
No 8   Bridesmaid's basket.
No 9   Open work oval basket.
No 10 Very modern oval basket with unusual handle.
No 11 Square-based basket constructed in thin wood strips.

WHITE VASES

No 1 Modern thin-necked bottle vase.
No 2 Handkerchief vase.
No 3 Flat-based measure or jug.
No 4 Very modern tazza on a foot.
No 5 Crystal bowl on a slender stem.
No 6 Small crystal vase.
No 7 Round soup tureen with lid.
No 8 Decanter vase.
No 9 Shallow shell-like bowl.
No 10 Modern posy trough in different shapes.

CONTAINERS

A variety of containers can be used to hold flowers. Vases, tankards, jugs, urns, mugs, dishes, caskets, baskets and cups to name a few. Some will hold water, others such as trays, some baskets and plates will be used in conjunction with a container which will not show, but just hold the flowers—this container is hidden by surrounding it with stones, moss, etc. Care must be taken to ensure that the water does not siphon onto the moss, and from there over onto a surface which it can damage.

Remember that the flowers and container form an overall picture. An arrangement cannot be carried out without taking the container into consideration—if it has not to show, then the surrounding features make up the picture, e.g. a large spreading group over a fireplace makes use of the surrounds in the overall picture. The arrangement on its own would be nothing. In this book these points will be emphasised many times. Colour, the type of container and different flowers all need to be carefully considered to get the best effect. The vase must be the correct size, not too large or too small, so as to get just the right balance—visual and actual. The addition of objet d'art at the side of an arrangement can make all the difference to the picture in terms of visual balance. The pictures on pages 40, 42 and 44 show a range of containers which allow for all sorts of arrangements. Some can be used for all occasions and with all kinds of flowers, for example: clear and slightly tinted glass, plain black and white ceramics, pottery, brass, copper, pewter, copper-tinted, bronze-green or stone coloured containers, together with baskets of all types in cane work, willow and chipwood, harmonise at home with many flowers and interiors. However, brightly coloured and richly decorated vases detract attention from the arrangement and must be used with great care. Certain shapes and materials make a vase more suitable for a particular type of arrangement, an old-fashioned style of arrangement is more suitable in a heavy bronze urn; a modern-style composition in a long glass or stainless steel cylinder or perhaps a futuristic ceramic shape.

It is useful for the amateur to collect all kinds of containers, thereby allowing a wide choice from which to choose when arranging flowers. Good vases can make valuable decorative pieces on their own, when flowers are expensive during the winter months.

RENANTHERA
Spider Orchids

Tom Thumb is the name given to a modern, thin-necked, long glass vase such as the one illustrated with spider orchids in it. The shape and colour of these small orchids on long wiry stems, is attractive. To some people they appear as large insects and for that reason are not always popular. The depth of colour at the centre is supplied by golden lilies and yellow snapdragons. The stems appear to have been placed at random, but care has been taken to get the curving stems over the front of the vase. These orchids, which originate from Singapore, are long lasting, anything up to three weeks if they have travelled well and quickly from their homeland.

LONG LASTING FLOWERS

A very modern vase is used for this arrangement of lilies, Ranunculus and daffodil buds. It is set against a background of white and grey, giving a silvery effect to the reflections. The flower colourings are a mixture of yellows and copper tones. The arrangement is made by first fixing the willow stem in the right hand side, the lily buds giving the height. The other stems are then used, threaded through the small opening, allowing the open Ranunculus to bend over the rim at the front of the container.

46

Materials to give decorative effects

To create extra interest or to give a personal touch to an arrangement, various pieces of decorative interest may be added to a group. Candles for example, make all the difference to table arrangements and Christmas decorations with their many styles and colours—the flowers being arranged around them with care to avoid a fire hazard. Dried stems and roots, denuded of their bark, bleached and polished make a very striking addition to a modern composition. Fruit, worked into a group, can add colour and brightness to the flowers.

Sometimes extra effects are used to help hold the arrangement firmly or to conceal the mechanics, oasis or pinholder, which if showing, spoil the result. For this purpose, rocks, stones of unusual shape, shells, moss, cork bark, bark covered with lichen and ribbon can be used advantageously. Small pieces of china, or statues, linking the style of the arrangement, and to be very modern, the addition of feathers or butterflies can all help to add to the overall effect as long as it is done with good taste.

VENICE

Nothing is more pleasing than to arrange your flowers where they are to be displayed. Use a dustsheet around the vase to collect the rubbish and avoid making a mess. First consider which container is to be used, bearing in mind the flowers and the background, which will all add to the overall effect. The size of the materials and the colouring will guide you in your choice of container. In the arrangement—'Venice', a valuable modern vase, 18" high and 2½" x 2½" of green and blue shades has been chosen to hold tulips, Forsythia, and a single stem of a fine-leafed Camellia. The tulips have been encouraged to take up interesting curves by manipulation.

COLOURED EMBROIDERY

Fragile stems of lilies in shades of orange, yellow and pink, have been chosen to make this arrangement. Because a delicate effect was required, the anthers have been left on the lilies, which gives them a lighter appearance. The beautiful rose 'Madame A. Meilland', so elegant in bud and full bloom, adds the extra weight and colour necessary at the base. A very modern, flat, square container holds the flowers.

This would make a magnificent picture painted or embroidered on pale silk, giving an impression of balance and peace.

FIRST OF MAY

A rectangular earthenware container on a raised base has been chosen for this spring arrangement. The flowers are held by a moss-covered pin-holder fitted into the back of the vase base. Branches of Malus in full bloom give the height. Lily of the valley on its roots is tucked below the Malus for support, and the base is finished with small clusters of white double daisies with tightly quilled petals. The remaining areas are covered with moss.

Gifts accompanied by flowers

Instead of sending a gift on its own, or a gift and flowers separately for a birthday, an engagement or a wedding, it is a nice idea to accompany the present, whatever it may be, with beautifully presented flowers attached to it. Choose the flowers to suit the occasion and size of the present. A piece of jewellery placed into a cellophane box containing a beautiful corsage, or a simple kitchen utensil with an attractive bunch of flowers attached to it and tied with a ribbon, are simple ways of enhancing the presentation of a gift.

THE PLEASURE OF GIVING
Violets are not now so fashionable. (This is probably because we can no longer get the beautiful Parma Violets from abroad, and most of those grown are short stemmed and without scent.) However, what could be nicer and more touching than to give an arrangement of violets to our grandparents, reminding them of happy days of their youth, long ago. Small, pale green opaline caskets are ideal for arranging these delicately perfumed flowers in small clusters, together with a few sprays of mimosa. Unfortunately, neither of these flowers is long lasting. The large snow-white pearls of the Symphoricarpos will lighten the arrangement when it is completed.

49

WICKER BASKET OF ROSES

A finely worked white wicker basket with a high handle, filled with light red polyantha roses in a simple and haphazard fashion. The full flowers convey the wealth of summer without appearing too heavy. The arrangement has a certain grace about it and the natural foliage adds to its beauty.

This type of rose is difficult to arrange in any way, because the individual flower stems are so short. The basket could either contain a bowl with wire netting, or a block of oasis with a polythene lining.

SWEET PEAS

These delicate, light and scented flowers always attract attention. They have such lovely fresh colours. In the picture at the top of this page, two vases of different colours are coupled together—one white and one brown, to make the modern container. The flower stems rise from a cluster of foliage in delicate sprays, the Dracaena, Croton and Maranta leaves contain colours which tie up with those of the flowers and give weight to the arrangement, without detracting from the main decorative effect of the sweet peas.

CONTRAST

On a marble mantelpiece in a room with period furnishings, a very modern rectangular vase in slate colouring has been chosen for this arrangement. In contrast, at its side, lies a flimsy grey-blue scarf. The flowers are Epidendrons, orchids, Gerbera and Anthuriums, with a rosette of Crypthanthus leaves on the left hand side and bare branches forming a structure of broken lines, vertical, oblique and horizontal, which go to create an unusual design.

The contradicting lines of the arrangement and the lightness of the orchid sprays give the arrangement a pleasing yet an amateurish touch.

THE ROSE DANCERS

A fascinating summer design of roses and white Antirrhinums against a background of virginia creeper.

It was created for an engagement party. The entwined branches found in the forest have been carefully bleached and manipulated with great skill by the inspired artist, who sees in them dancers or even the image of a couple. This remarkable piece of wood work forms the main structure of the arrangement and the flowers are carefully worked through it. The container holding the flowers is not seen, being placed behind the branches. The whole group stands at table level.

ELEGANCE

Three crystal goblets on slender stems are standing in tiers in a straight line. These are holding a few elegant stems of flowering Japanese azaleas and sprays of jasmine foliage. No netting or oasis is used in case it detracts from the pure sparkle of the clear water and glass. Only a few stems can be used in this carefully balanced light arrangement.

FIREWORKS

Twelve flowers of Anthurium andreanum of different size and colour and two branches of Croton, make up the richness and the glistening colours of this arrangement, rising from the satin finished glassware vase, the fluting similar to that of the Anthurium spathes.

Each flower is really an inflorescence—rather like a modified corn cob. The spadix rises out of a large bract or spathe, which lasts a long time. These unusual flowers, often lasting a month, are suited to modern style decorations, coming in different colours from scarlet red to white and all of them very dramatic.

FLORAL PIPETTE

This Austrian pipette is meant to contain white wine and be placed on the dining table, so that guests can help themselves during a meal. It is arranged here with the much appreciated long-stemmed garden roses named 'Queen Elizabeth'. These go well with the curiously marked poppy seed heads and the wrought iron stand.

CHINESE PÆONIES
(Opposite)

A low Chinese table on which is standing a vase of the same origin containing a large arrangement of pæonies in a range of colours. These are simply arranged in wire netting with nothing other than their own foliage to break the strong colours. They are quite long lasting if cut when in bud and allowed plenty of water.

The table, vase and flowers bring to mind the Far East from where they all originated.

A HAT FROM INDONESIA

Although this appears as a basket in the picture, it is really a hat lying in the garden on a flagstone. It contains long pink-coloured Antirrhinum and bright yellow, round flower heads of Achillea. The yellow colour comes through the arrangement as a very strong band of colour. The basket holds oasis and wire netting wrapped in polythene and is finished off with ties of matching coloured cotton tape.

A SCREEN OF ANNUAL DELPHINIUMS

Wood again features in this bank of flowers. It is extremely lavish, and could only be carried out at the height of the summer when these flowers are easily obtainable. Gnarled wood, probably a large stem of tree ivy, scrubbed but left in a natural state, depicts, according to the artist, an animal on the watch.

The whole thing is constructed in blocks of oasis in well hidden shallow tins. The strong blues and pinks are highlighted with a few white larkspur. Provided the water level is maintained, the flowers should be long-lasting.

A MODERN ARRANGEMENT

The container for this arrangement is a white earthenware vase with two apertures. It is filled with 11 'Interflora' roses, 2 Sansevieria leaves, a piece of bleached root and a few stems of willow, which is just breaking into leaf. The arrangement is constructed as follows: first get the height by fixing the two leaves from the Sansevieria in a bold line at the highest point of the vase. This will contrast with the willow and root at the base of the first group. Remove some of the foliage from the roses to create a light and airy effect, allowing 8 flowers in the top aperture. The remaining 3 go in at an angle in the lower group. The stems of young weeping willow add width to the overall arrangement and tend to bring together the two separate arrangements.

MASTERPIECE

This original work tries to combine expressive line with the beauty of flowers in warm colourings, and illustrates the vivacity of living things. The lilies stand erect next to the brown 'thorns' on the bare branches. Each group is set in a stoneware container in the shape of a flat cup, the pinholder supporting the stems being covered with moss or pebbles.

A WEALTH OF CARNATIONS

The value of this group is enhanced by the container in which the flowers are arranged. The tall slim stem and wide mouth allows freedom in using many flowers in a large display. In our picture we have 'Nora Sim' carnations, in both single flowers and spray form, which last extremely well and are obtained from the South of France. Sprays of Eucalyptus cinerea add beauty and line to this group.

The whole group is worked in oasis covered with wire netting for support. Many types of flowers and foliage could be used in a container of this type.

BARBEQUE

This is a bit of nonsense but would add fun to the occasion. Suitable for a house-warming party when it could contain all types of flowers, fruit and even vegetables in a merry and attractive arrangement.

On this occasion, sun flowers and hollyhocks, Gaillardias and garlic add brightness and interest to the collection in the garden. To arrange this successfully, some long stemmed flowers are necessary because the water container or oasis fits on the shelf at flower level.

SCULPTURED TORTOISE

This bulky tree stump was discovered whilst out for a walk in the forest. It was carried home and with a little sculpturing, made into this curious tortoise which now decorates a lawn. With some careful additions the whole animal can be brightened up, as seen in the picture on this page. It appears here to be leaving its shelter of golden privet and scarlet dahlias, the brightness of which stress its unusual character.

EREMURUS

A group of pale pink Eremurus, 3'–5' high, and dark pink lupins arranged in an old, upright, copper-coloured watering can.

Eremurus flower around the end of May to early June. A tall lily from central Asia, very useful in large arrangements or as background border plants, where they seem to dominate all other plants. They are not easy to use because of their very thick stem and the weight of the open flower spike. They should be cut with a sharp knife and placed in water straight away. The flowers open from the bottom of the spike and work upwards. By removing the lower flowers as they die, the upper ones will be encouraged to develop and open, so extending the life of the flower spike.

GIFT WITH FLOWERS

This flat Venetian candlestick has been gaily decorated as a present. The colours of the flowers have been carefully chosen to set off the clear yellow glass ring. Stems of Zinnia, Ranunculus, berries of whitebeam and small crab apples with purple Berberis, go to make the arrangement. The blue colouring is obtained from Veronica and a little Campanula. If small flowers were not available, the candlestick top could hold a red or blue candle equally well.

TEA ON THE GRASS

This is a real nonsense and could be anything a young child might think up. It appears as three collections of summer flowers which have been stood in Picasso pottery containers on the grass, and these pots are not really suited to flowers. The actual flowers are good, white Agapanthus, Phlox, small Dahlia, Campanula, Scabious and Liatris. The large, flat Megasia leaves are completely wasted. It is a collection of material rather than an arrangement.

DEBUT

A glass bird appears to live in the shelter of five stems of Lara rose, Freesia and spiky citrus branches (Poncirus trifoliata). There is a touch of originality about this composition. Instead of the usual cradle of flowers, it could be used to celebrate the arrival of a new baby.

AUTUMN ROSES

A simple arrangement of 'Queen Elizabeth' roses at the end of the season. Many of the half-open buds will extend the flowering period in the home. The Virginia creeper certainly will not last long—once coloured, to this extent, the leaves will very soon drop.

The colourings of the foliage and flowers blend well with those on the old Strasburg Pitcher, and make a pleasing picture set in the chimney corner.

ARISTOCRACY

An arrangement supposed to represent two parent birds standing over a nest of youngsters awaiting their food. The Strelitzia are very bird-like and commonly known as the 'Bird of Paradise'. They have curious orange and blue flowers springing from a beak-like structure and seem to associate animal life with plant life in the perfectly structured and stable arrangement. The three Seku seed pods are also unusual in their structure and can well be likened to open beaks awaiting food from the birds above. The stems of Dizygotheca elegantissima with their finely cut leaves and the looped Djangara leaves make a good contrast to this striking arrangement.

CASCADE OF FLOWERS

This is a clever arrangement in a flat brown earthenware dish, made from grasses, slender branches of pink Japanese azalea, two Cryptanthus plants, some distorted roots and moss.

It is made as follows: fix a pinholder to the base of the dish and cover with wire netting which will automatically give weight to the arrangement. Split a bamboo cane and fix to the back, making the necessary height. Into this place the fronds of dried grass carefully, displaying them in such a way as to hide the cane. At set places secure small water-filled glass tubes in which to display the Azalea—this again carefully done so that it does not show in any way. At the foot, place the roots, which will give the appearance of a solid support to the arrangement.

This would need constant watching to see that the water tubes remain full.

SMALL ROMANTIC BOUQUETS

Small round or fan-shaped bunches are always popular. They can be used in many ways—as a decoration on a table or as presents at place settings for the ladies at a dinner; and again as a child's gift to mother on Mothers' Day.

The one in bright oranges, yellows and reds, made from lilliput Zinnias and small shoots of variegated Veronica, goes well with the vase, tomatoes and ribbons. On the flat wicker platter filled with plums, lies a gay bunch of blue cornflowers, pink miniature roses ('Montserrat Pearls') and deep pink larkspur, tied with a velvet ribbon.

Each season brings a variety of small flowers from which a never-ending selection of bunches can be made up, and which usually last a long time. If correctly made they can just stand up in a small vase as a decoration, and need not be untied.

RAYONANTHE CHRYSANTHEMUMS (Page 65).

An excellent rounded Madoura vase in polished ceramic which looks good against a stone setting. The well-positioned flowers in white, yellow and pale orange have a few leaves of Rhoeo to add interest to the arrangement, which is simple, clean cut and well suited to standing on the ground in front of the stone wall.

SUMMER SYMPHONY

Straight, square and round vases in various sizes holding plenty of water are most useful for flower arrangements. They can also be in various colours, but white and black vases go with most flowers.

In this arrangement, the white goes well with the yellow, orange and white flowers. The arrangement is made around two stout bamboo canes, set at different lengths and slightly apart. The tall yellow lily is 'Golden Clarion'. The spotted lily at the centre, Lilium tigrinum 'Splendens', gracefully gives a little width to the arrangement and the cream Tokyo sprays add their lightness to the splendour of the lilies. The ribbons in matching colours add finish to the decoration.

COCKSCOMB

This is the first time I can ever remember seeing this flower set in an arrangement. In fact, I have never seen cockscomb growing as tall as this before. Here they are arranged in a copy of an antique pitcher with sprays of Cotoneaster in full berry and two branches of young walnut fruits on branches. A few fruits rest at the base. A clever, well-arranged group for an autumn arrangement.

SHIMMERING COLOURS

A good title for the very set style of this arrangement of orange lilies and yellow Tokyo spray. No leaves or stems are showing in order to give full colour value to the group. Set in an upright white vase, the whole value of this type of arrangement is in its bright colours blending together. It is extravagant on flowers.

ULTRA-MODERN PRESENTATION

It is difficult to really describe this decoration. Two rectangular steel containers, set at different angles hide the pots of two growing cacti—all that can be seen of them are the bulbous tops looking like sea urchins. Between them, vases hold stems of perfect Nerine, in the brightest of scarlet, and one leafless branch which could be a Cornus or something of similar habit.

To add to its originality, white silk fringes have been draped over the lower flowers. This avant-garde composition is only suited to a very modern setting—the person who designed it suggests a sideboard in the home of a newly married couple. Although containing very little material, those used would be very expensive.

WINTRY DANCE

An apple tree trunk with branches attached, makes the basic foundation for this clever flower arrangement. The flowers are few but well-placed, and as such, they symbolise late autumn amongst the dead material which represents the winter to come. The Leucodendron (or pincushion flowers) and stem of Pavao-Klein are South African, the other materials, Cotoneaster and virginia creeper leaves, grow at home. All are fitted into damp oasis attached to the trunk and well disguised.

TEMPTATION

Is the impression gained from this luxurious, well-balanced arrangement in a very heavy pottery vase. It contains some exotic material, such as Protea, pineapple, Heliconia, together with other very decorative materials—Anthurium, auratum and longiflorum lilies, Dracaena and dried Gynerium leaves, so it is not a cheap arrangement to copy. It could be changed by using easily obtainable flowers in the same style.

DELICATE ORCHIDS

A vase in the shape of a hand, gracefully carries inflorescences of Cymbidium and dainty Phalenopsis orchids, which flow through a cluster of small Cryptanthus and fronds of a young fern in pale green. The beauty of curves has been carefully studied in this arrangement.

FRUIT AND FLOWERS

This arrangement, rich in colour, makes a delightful group of fruit and flowers. Standing against the window, it is in full light, which is reflected in the fruits.

It has been constructed on blocks of oasis, covered with netting and held together on a bamboo frame which has been fixed firmly in the wicker basket. For safety, I would also suggest the top of the support be secured to the window frame, to help balance the whole arrangement, which when completed would be quite heavy. The flowers are long lasting, and providing the oasis is kept really damp, should not require attention for a few days.

In the arrangement are fresh Protea, white Gerbera and Gloriosa. The fruits are a fresh pineapple, green and red apples, and black and green grapes. The whole thing is brought together with bows of blue and brown ribbon and some flowering stems of Ruscus foliage.

WICKERWORK TRAY

The autumn foliage, Mahonia and virginia creeper already turned purple by the first chilly days are very decorative. Their hues of copper, russet and red are ideal together with Gerbera and sprays of Euphorbia fulgens arranged in this wicker tray. The flowers are set slightly to one side to allow for seasonal fruits, in this case, pomegranates and grapes. It is finished with bleached broom sprays and a naturally curving stem of Malus to balance the arrangement.

A DECORATED PIECE OF FURNITURE

An artistic arrangement of fruit and flowers for a July reception. This antique table has two containers filled with flowers, giving a still life effect. The two types of onion; Allium giganteum and Allium albopilosum, have small starry flowers, yellow Achillea and Gaillardia in brown-red make up the flowers used in the group, together with pineapples, melons, grapefruit, lemons and cherries. The fresh materials go into wet oasis held by wire netting. The pineapples have been fixed to a bamboo stake and follow the line of the Allium stems. The colours of the flowers and fruit, chosen with taste, give the arrangement an air of lightness and simplicity.

FRUIT BOWL
(Opposite)

A glorious and unusual arrangement of 3 pineapples with multi-coloured leaves, 2 sugar canes, 2 pomegranates, a cob of sweet corn, 2 figs, 2 lemons and limes, 2 peaches, 1 apple, 1 white squash, green nuts; a few heads of Achillea and sprays of Gloriosa—the flame lily, complete the group.

This is the type of arrangement one longs to make on arriving in foreign parts, where these items are so cheap and plentiful—one can only admire this type of group from pictures if living in this country, unless a very good friend brings such things home as a present!

It is constructed as follows: pieces of dry oasis make a platform on which to rest the fruits, and two containers with wet oasis to hold the fresh materials are fitted into the back of the bowl.

First securely fix the sugar cane at the correct height and angles, then the pineapples. These are wired carefully to the netting and are not in water. Build up the fruits to hold firmly, arranging colours and shapes to show to good advantage. Lastly, fit in the wet oasis, the stems of the gloriosa lily and fill the last gaps in with the small light fruits and dry Achillea. These fruits, mostly exotic, roots and flowers, form a long-lasting composition which will immediately attract the attention of guests at a party. In the photograph, carved chinese sticks have been added in places to give it an unusual effect.

VERTICAL STYLE AUTUMN ARRANGEMENT

A few sprays of golden rod at three distinct levels set the outline of this group, and numerous cactus dahlias set out the strong and erect main line. The richly coloured flowers and neat vase stand out against the background which certainly makes them show to good advantage. The very nature of the slender vase has influenced the style of the arrangement which in normal conditions would be considered unbalanced and out of proportion.

AN ARRANGEMENT OF THE FUTURE

Here is a bold arrangement with flowing lines forecasting the style of the next ten years? A beautiful, slim, tall vase harmonises perfectly with the arrangement.

With good proportions, well balanced and denuded of superfluous foliage, it charms

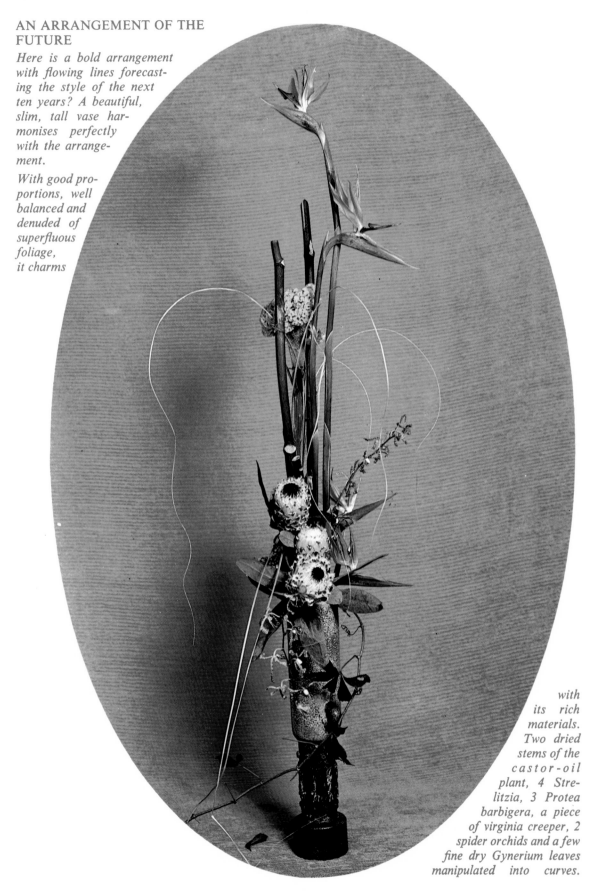

with its rich materials. Two dried stems of the castor-oil plant, 4 Strelitzia, 3 Protea barbigera, a piece of virginia creeper, 2 spider orchids and a few fine dry Gynerium leaves manipulated into curves.

WALL DECORATION

*At receptions and cocktail parties, guests stand around, and any flowers arranged on tables or at
ground level are not seen once the room begins to fill with people. On these occasions,
wall decorations are very useful because they may be seen by everybody.
In the picture we have an excellent decoration which has been constructed as follows with
very choice materials:
It is important not to deface the wall fabric, so great care must be given to the backing
of the wall bracket. In this case, oasis has been covered with netting and wired to a piece of
cork bark. The stems of flowers and foliage have been stuck into the oasis. In some cases it
may be necessary to wire the pieces to make them stand out well and at the correct angle, but
careful selection of materials will usually overcome this problem. Against an orange
background we have Strelitzia, variegated pineapple and palm foliage, sprays of orange
coloured pimento, Heliconia, Pomegranate, Protea and single orange and yellow Chrysanthemums.*

BACK FROM HUNTING

Back from hunting is the title given to this group, but I would prefer it used as a decoration for a shooting party. As this composition shows, game can form a valuable part of a big decoration; especially pheasants with their superbly coloured plumage.

Cleverly displayed, these pheasants appear to fall onto a heap of scattered fruits, flowers and autumn leaves, matching well with their feathers. The choice of materials for this arrangement is Physalis, perennial sunflowers, dahlias, Pæony and virginia creeper foliage, stems of Cotinus, Ampelodesma grasses and the odd dead branch.

The arrangement is made in a flat dish with oasis and wire netting—a metal support is used to bear the top bird, carefully disguised by clever placing of the top stems.

The
enchantment
of summer

branch of contorted willow. The title of this composition 'Tortured Spirit' is apt.

A few Strelitzias from a florist shop combined with some Chrysanthemums, give an artistic touch to 'Birds of Paradise'. During the Harvest season, when flowers begin to become scarce in the garden, mix them with fruits and berries—rose hips in our picture, to add value to the decoration. In 'A Gleam of Autumn' the vine branches about to lose their yellow leaves, the briar branches with brilliant red berries and wild clematis, picked from the hedgerow whilst out walking, reflect the warmth of the last rays of sunshine; whilst 'In the Hearth' brings to mind all the forest glowing with its golden brightness. Around a few stems of Proteas and lilies, 'Temptation' unfurls.

Supple and gracious lines formed by tortured willow, wired flowers and rosettes of Cryptanthus, cleverly attached

Southern Cross   Take off

88

Temptation

to branches, a stem of spider orchids and fern fronds, are all well set up in a modern vase. 'Southern Cross' is the title given to this formal presentation bouquet which gets its beauty from the warm colours of the flowers from which it has been made, namely: orange lilies, spider chrysanthemums, blue Iris and chinese lanterns, all brought together with leaves in loops looking like ribbon. 'Summer Enchantment' is the result of gathering a wide range of flowers together—those of the late spring, through summer, to the early autumn. In 'Sweetness of Anjou', the dark green stylish branches of broom form an outline for the delicate hues of the Ranunculus and polyantha roses. 'Take Off' is an apt name for the group at the bottom of page 88. The container plays an important part in this arrangement—the round lid contrasting with the tall stalks of the Delphinium. A few ordinary flowers, soft-hued roses and single Asters finish off the base.

Sweetness of Anjou   In the hearth

89

Birds of paradise

A gleam of autumn

GRAND STAIRCASE

A large white Medici vase, 28" in height, has been chosen to
decorate this stately staircase. The vase, of simple shape, is easy
to arrange because it has a wide top and is well balanced.
The flowers chosen are white Gladioli and Bermuda
lilies, yellow orangy and brick-red Chrysanthemums,
and branches of Ruscus foliage.

90

Modern simplicity

Prestige

Fugue

Flower decorated baskets

Receptions

Standing on a glass topped table, three separate arrangements in long stemmed crystal goblets go to make the group. Striking copper coloured Gerbera, delicate Cypripediums and long, arching, slender stems of Euphorbia, blend in harmony of shape and colour. Good lighting conditions will show this sophisticated arrangement off to its best advantage.

DUCK WITH ORANGE

A round table ready for a few guests is decorated with an original and attractive table centre. The table cloth with large stylish flowers and bright colourings inspired the idea for this arrangement. A green pottery container in the form of a dish with a duck-shaped lid, is used to hold the marigolds. These are placed at different angles and are of different lengths, so as to be seen by the guests from all sides. The oranges in halves, provide a different lustre, and having clean cut lines, add to the decorative effect.

Flowers impart a sense of gaiety and luxury to the table setting. They should not, however, cause any inconvenience when the table is laid for a meal—the arrangement must be kept to a correct size for the table. Normally the height should not prevent the guests from seeing one another, and an average of about 10″ is usually correct. So much depends on the occasion. At some very fine Royal banquets I have seen arrangements of over 3′ in height, placed down the centre of the large tables! The size and shape of the vase and arrangement, will vary with that of the table. A round vase being suited to a round table, oval or oblong vases to the long styled tables. For a table seating 4–6 guests, one fairly small central arrangement would be enough. For a large oblong table it may be a good idea to have a valuable china centre piece, or some other special feature and to each side of it at a little distance, a flower decoration, tying up with it in some way. In the absence of the special central item, make three arrangements; the middle one could be larger and of more importance, or all three could match.

Table arrangements

Normally candles are not used for luncheon parties and the flower decorations are a little simpler than those used for dinner, when the elegance of candles adds to the arrangement which can be more elaborate. One idea consists of taking a table cloth with coloured flower design and using the same flowers and colours for the arrangement. See the 'Duck with Orange' photograph on page 93.

In the drawing room, where coffee is served, one or two medium sized decorations are sufficient. On this occasion, provided it suits the interior decoration colours, use blues, violets or lemon yellows which lose their value in artificial light so are often not at their best at night. Colour can vary so much under different lights that this must be given careful consideration.

For a dinner, even greater care must be taken in arranging the flowers, because the time taken over the meal is so much longer, thereby giving the guest more time to study, admire or criticise the arrangements!

The flowers and the vase should be changed all the time. Make use of pretty vases in crystal and coloured glass, silver, pewter and delicate china. Light and brightly coloured flowers will often show up well in artificial light, and can look good in candlelight.

Flowers just placed on the table (out of water) to extend the decoration, must be of good quality and perfectly fresh, so that they last without wilting. They are best placed in little groups, as posies. This idea is not really appreciated by flower lovers, because they prefer that the flowers always are in water, so if you wish to make use of this idea, do so at the last minute before the guests arrive. Remove surplus water from the stems so that the table surface is not damaged.

A COUNTRY LUNCH TABLE SETTING
(Opposite)

Table decorations for a plain polished table in a country home. The table is set with glazed ovenware from the Islettes (Meuse), XVIIIth and XIXth centuries.

The arrangements consist of snapdragons in red, yellow and white, yellow Achillea filipendulina, mauve Erigeron, sweet william, oats and green wheat. Old china decorated with flowers has been chosen for the lunch party.

The reflections in the dark wood multiply and bring out the colours of the china and those of the flowers. The decorated soup tureen is used for the table centre piece. The rich flower colours harmonize with the colour in the china to give a bright and friendly welcome to the guests.

GARDEN PARTY

Flowers used in this oblong shaped blue and white dish are marguerites, cornflowers, perennial sunflowers, small Eryngium and seed heads of sorrel. A cross-stitch table cloth in the colourings of the chosen flowers and a piece of blue and white china adds to the overall effect. The stems of the uneven groups are held on pinholders concealed by short flowers and flower heads. A natural and simple country-style decoration blending well with the country setting in which it is placed.

95

Balls—Grand receptions

Although really large balls are somewhat rare nowadays, it is still interesting to imagine how one could approach the task of florally decorating the ballroom and surrounding rooms, as, from time to time, such occasions still do occur.

If the ball were to be held in a country house set in its own grounds then it is likely that the trees beside the drive leading up to the house would be floodlit, setting the scene for the festivities inside. On the steps leading up to the door four giant candelabra on pillars frame the main entrance. The candelabra are filled with many candles and garlanded with flowers and leaves.

The choice of flowers for such receptions varies, of course, with the season. Tulips are most useful, especially for town functions, since they can be purchased from December until mid-May. The range of colours is unending and they also combine well with many other flowers.

In June, roses also give a wide selection of colours but do not always mix well with other species, and they are often better on their own. Roses can look superb in a drawing room or as a table decoration. Very large arrangements can be built up from spring flowering shrubs such as branches of Forsythia, lilac, cherry and Malus or Prunus triloba and sprays of wichuraiana roses will supply marvellous outline shapes. Tulips, Pæonies, Irises, lupins, Delphiniums, Eremerus, Gladioli and hollyhocks all go well with the shrubs.

In Autumn the choice of Michaelmas daisies is a boon to the floral artist creating large displays. Other Autumn flowers available include Dahlias, sunflowers, Solidago and many other species too.

At a reception one or two well-lit and beautiful groups are better than several small arrangements. Concealed spot lighting is ideal for these decorations. If possible each group should tone in with the interior décor and furnishings. To begin with, an arrangement of vividly coloured flowers in the entrance hall will welcome the guests and immediately put them at ease, encouraging a relaxed atmosphere. In the main hall, where two brightly coloured, matching groups standing six feet high, glitter under the lights within the well-illuminated reception room, the host and hostess receive their guests, backed by a floral decoration whose colours pick up those of the hostess' dress.

The ballroom will be lit by a series of wall-bracket lights garnished with baubels, flowers and ribbons and be decorated by six or eight arrangements on pedestals. These arrangements should be light yet elegant and can be lit by carefully concealed spot lights. The adjoining drawing rooms can have their furniture covered in green, yellow or red material, according to the colour of the curtains and awnings. In these rooms the flowers will be more striking if the theme of one colour is maintained throughout.

Later on in the evening, the doors of the dining room are flung back for the guests to enter for supper, which will be eaten at small tables covered with dark red table cloths. On each table a candlestick holding four candles provides the only light in the room, and the base of the candlestick holder is garlanded with red flowers and foliage.

COUNTRY ARRANGEMENT
Dutch style—XVIth century

Flowers are used in profusion, overflowing from the vase and cascading in all directions. Poppies, Rhododendron, lilac, garden pinks, ox-eye daisy, Allium, cornflowers, sage, Arabis, roses, stocks, pansies, Iris, columbine, Malus—all these late spring flowers have been put together in all their beauty to please the eye.

They are arranged in a Sèvres vase, which contains wire netting and also three flower tubes or cones built into the framework to hold the short stemmed flowers. A little wire or oasis is in these tubes.

It is important to remember to keep the shape of the vase when working in sections, and to vary the colours in a balanced fashion. Start with the top first and get a framework planned, then fix the width, in this case with the silver-grey Stachys lanata foliage at regular intervals. Now start to fill the gaps with the numerous touches of colour, using the various flowers of different lengths. Although really a facing arrangement the vase has fullness at the front and sides so that it may be viewed with interest from several angles.

Celebrations and special occasions

WELCOME

A very modern three-tier container to welcome guests, garnished with lemons, tangerines, oranges, grapefruit and chestnuts. The fruit is laid on glass marbles on each tier, which allows it to remain above the water, yet keep fresh, and at the same time firmly secure the Chrysanthemum worked into the arrangement. A bunch of white grapes cascades down the side, whilst a long stalked Chrysanthemum bloom gives a modern touch to the arrangement and at the same time attracts attention to the bird at the top of the vase.

With few flowers and plenty of fruit this is an easy and economical decoration to do in a few minutes when an unexpected guest arrives.

In town it is often difficult to obtain choice foliage, and the amateur who owns a garden would therefore do well to plant a large selection of plants capable of producing this foliage: Mahonia, Portuguese laurel, Aucuba, Cotoneasters in variety, broom, Eleagnus, Cornus, Berberis in variety, Bergenia, Hosta, Astrantia and Alchemilla to name a few. Leaves are always useful and help with the arrangement of most flowers. As already stated, it is often good to remove some of the leaves from flowers to help keep them, and in some cases to remove all, replacing these leaves with sprays of foliage where necessary to balance the arrangement.

Many occasions occur when it is necessary to decorate the house with flowers. The type of decoration will vary according to the circumstances.

To celebrate christenings or confirmation, white flowers will be used or very pale and fresh-coloured flowers. For special services, such as private communion, a wide choice of flowers is available from which to choose, to make a medium-sized attractive arrangement.

The tradition in France was to use white or pink flowers for engagements or weddings; this now appears to be disappearing except for the decoration in the church. It makes it easier for the person to decorate the house with flowers from the garden when not having to keep strictly to a colour. Only use pale colours and if possible, include some of the following classical flowers: Arum or other lilies, Freesia, roses, lilac, Stephanotis, carnations and orchids.

For silver and golden weddings, the colour of the container often denotes the special ceremony, a silver vase in the first case and a silver-gilt vase for the latter. The same applies to the flowers and foliage and even the ribbon added to finish the arrangement. I understand that long-bearded corn-cobs traditionally form a part of the arrangement in France—to date I have not come across any such thing in England.

For large cocktail and fork lunch parties, remove some of the furniture and make space for one or two large groups of flowers, to give atmosphere to the room. As many of the guests will remain standing, the groups should be on plinths, the vases well above the ground to show to advantage. Use well proportioned heavy vases that are firmly fixed and fill generously with flowers and foliage. On the buffet table, a four or five armed candelabra will look lovely filled with little posies of flowers. These candelabra may be hired in large towns from catering firms if not available from the family. Avoid overcrowding the candle holder with flowers in order to allow plenty of room for food on the buffet table. You can choose from a wide range of flowers, but remember however, that at evening parties, some colours do not look so good under artificial lights.

To celebrate recognition of some kind, for example, promotion in the Legion of Honour, red flowers should be used and depending on the season, choose from tulips, roses, Amaryllis or Anthurium.

For Mother's Day, a moveable date, but falling in the spring, obtain flowers with long lasting qualities. Many young people like to give presents of flowers and plants, such as bowls of bulbs, Hydrangea, polyanthus roses, Saintpaulia, or perhaps plants with coloured leaves: Dracaena, Croton. Sometimes cut flowers are worked in with these plants in a decoration called a 'pot et fleur'. When the cut flowers have died, the plants carry on to become a lasting memory of a child's love.

ENGAGEMENT
(*Silk Flowers*)

The dry flowers arrangements, of which our ancestors were so proud, and which we irreverently called 'dust collectors', are out of fashion, but for the last fifteen years or so, groups made up of natural dried flowers, grasses and seed heads, bleached or coloured are again in favour, due particularly to the large selection now available from either wild or cultivated indigenous or exotic plants from around the world.

After the silky and uninteresting plumes of pampas grasses standing alone in tall vases in bygone days, seemingly architecturally arranged groups took their place using many seed heads, curiously shaped and distorted roots and twigs, large and narrow leaves, spathes, hard and rigid shells, and fruits of all kinds; leaving the florist scope for imagination in the construction of both large and small decorations to enhance the interiors of modern homes, offices, shop windows and public halls.

Dry materials, at least those of exotic origin, are rather expensive but last a very long time. Not only do they last for months or years, but they can be changed from one arrangement to another.

Dry arrangements require little care, they should just be kept free from dust as far as possible. They will stand up to overheated rooms or cold rooms in winter, and remain well in places with little light, or in the full sun in the window. Actually it is true to say that they do become a little brittle after long periods in a very dry atmosphere and do fade a little in a bright light, but this is a very gradual process. They please over a very long time, similar to a painting or a piece of sculpture! This explains, and justifies the high price which is asked for some arrangements.

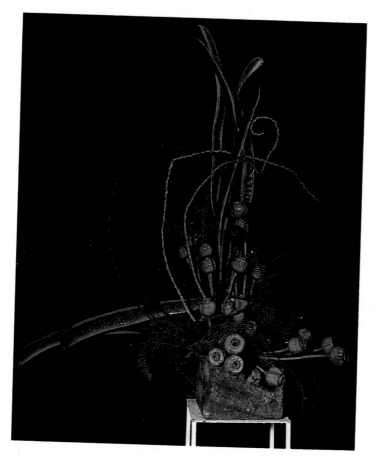

MODERN CONTRAST OF GREEN AND BLUES
A vertical style

Thirty poppy heads, painted blue, and used at the base of this arrangement, set in a modern, square, heavy, grey-blue container, adds a splash of colour beneath a few green winding sapha branches, coral fern leaves, and the long pointed acacia pods which set the height of the group.

AN UNUSUAL GARDEN

A plant trough on short legs has been used for this modern design. The dried materials for this arrangement have been placed into blocks of oasis held firmly by large rounded stones. The large white flowers are three whitened artichokes, backed by tall white branches and brown-red seed heads of Salvia. The red-painted poppy seed heads give a splash of colour at the base of the group. Certainly a different arrangement from the usual plant trough.

IMAGINATION

A good title for this very difficult, modern, apple-green container with its 2" aperture to one side of the top of the vase. It is just wide enough to hold these striking dried materials, some hand painted and man-made, and other drieds which are now becoming so popular. Unfortunately they are given various names by the manufacturers and it is difficult to identify all of them.

The following pages show
collections of seed pods, dried
flowers, leaves, fruits and branches,
many of which at present are not
available in the United Kingdom
but are shown here to encourage
people to collect as and when they
are able to obtain them.

Pages 107–109 do show many
dried flowers and foliages from the
garden which are well worth
saving, and have so often in the

past been used to start a bonfire.
A wide selection of seed pods
including the following: giant
coconut palm, Hakea, Jacaranda,
Acacia, cotton tree, lotus, beech
nuts, Eucalyptus, Sterculia,
Bignonia and bamboo.

*Here we have 18 different
types of Protea:*

Again another group of even more
exotic materials which are seldom
seen in this country. In fact only
the Sorghum, Heliconia, Banksia,
winged elm branch, Eucalyptus,
Hakea, poppy and baby wood
rose come to my mind, and then
I cannot remember whether it was
here or when abroad.

Drieds from the garden

This is a very different story and many of these things we can easily collect from the garden ourselves. Some seasons, of course, bring forth better dried materials, the less rain we have in the autumn, the better it is for materials, because they want to dry well on the plant before cutting.

1 Tulip
2 Lunaria (Honesty)
3 Stachys lanata
   (Lamb's ear flower stems)
4 Echinops (Globe thistle)
5 Centaurea
6/7/8 Allium (in different varieties)
9 Molucella (Bells of Ireland)

10 Eryngium (Sea holly)
11 Achillea (Yarrow)
12 Typha (Bullrush)

A guide to when flowers and bushes are available. This cannot be rigidly adhered to, because seasons do alter flowering times. Climatic conditions within the British Isles can also make a big difference, e.g. flowers from the south-west of England can be 4–6 weeks earlier than those

MONTHLY AVAILABILITY

Black line indicates available from the garden.

These times should be taken

Flower	J	F	M	A	M	J	J	A	S	O	N	D
Achillea filipendulina						█	█	█	█			
Acroclinium							█	█	█			
Adonis	█		█	█	█							
African Marigold							█	█				
Agapanthus						█	█	█				
Ageratum						█	█	█				
Allium				█	█							
Alstroemeria	█	█	█	█	█	█	█					
Amaranthus						█	█	█				
Amaryllis	█	█	█	█	█					█		
Anemone	█	█	█	█	█	█	█	█	█	█		
Anthemis						█	█	█				
Anthurium	█	█	█	█	█	█	█	█	█	█	█	█
Antirrhinum		█	█	█	█	█	█					
Arum		█	█	█	█	█	█					
Aster								█	█	█		
Aster callistephus							█	█	█	█		
Astilbe				█	█	█						
Azalea			█	█	█	█					█	
Bergenia		█	█	█								
Brompton Stock					█	█	█	█				
Buddleia							█	█	█			
Caladium				█	█							
Callicarpa									█	█	█	
Columbine					█	█	█					
Camellia		█	█	█	█	█					█	
Campanula						█	█	█	█			
Campanula (biennial)					█	█	█					
Campsis							█	█				
Carnation	█	█	█	█	█	█	█	█	█	█	█	█
Ceanothus					█	█						
Celosia							█	█				
Centaurea							█	█				
Chimonanthus	█	█										█
Chrysanthemum	█	█	█	█	█	█	█	█	█	█	█	█
Chrysanthemum (perennial)					█	█	█	█	█			
Clarkia						█	█	█				
Clematis						█	█					
Colchicum											█	█
Coreopsis						█	█	█				

Flower	J	F	M	A	M	J	J	A	S	O	N	D
Cornflower					█	█	█					
Cortaderia									█	█		
Cosmos								█	█	█		
Cotoneaster (berry)										█	█	█
Crocus	█	█										
Currant (flowering)		█	█	█								
Cyclamen	█	█	█	█						█	█	█
Cytisus					█	█						
Dahlia								█	█	█	█	
Daisy					█	█	█					
Daphne		█	█	█	█							
Delphinium					█	█	█	█				
Dicentra				█	█	█						
Echinops							█	█	█			
Eremurus						█	█					
Eucharis	█	█	█	█	█	█	█	█	█	█	█	█
Everlasting Flowers							█	█	█			
Flag Iris				█	█							
Forsythia	█	█	█									
Foxglove					█	█	█	█				
Freesia	█	█	█	█	█		█	█	█	█	█	█
French Marigold						█	█	█	█			
Fritillaria			█	█	█							
Fuchsia					█	█	█	█	█	█		
Gaillardia								█	█	█		
Gardenia	█	█	█	█	█	█	█	█	█	█	█	█
Gentian							█	█	█			
Gerbera	█	█	█	█	█	█	█	█	█	█	█	█
Geum					█	█	█					
Gladioli	█	█	█	█	█	█	█	█	█	█	█	█
Gloriosa									█	█		
Godetia					█	█	█					
Guelder Rose	█	█										
Gypsophila						█	█	█				
Helenium							█	█	█			
Helianthus							█	█	█			
Heliopsis							█	█	█			
Heliotrope						█	█	█	█			
Hellebore	█	█	█	█							█	█
Heuchera						█	█	█				

138

OF FLOWERS AND FRUITS

Red line indicates available from the Market and shops.

as a rough guide only.

from the north of England. Varieties also extend the season considerably, in some cases, e.g. Chrysanthemums and Anemones are in the market throughout the year and when dried, the season can be very much longer.

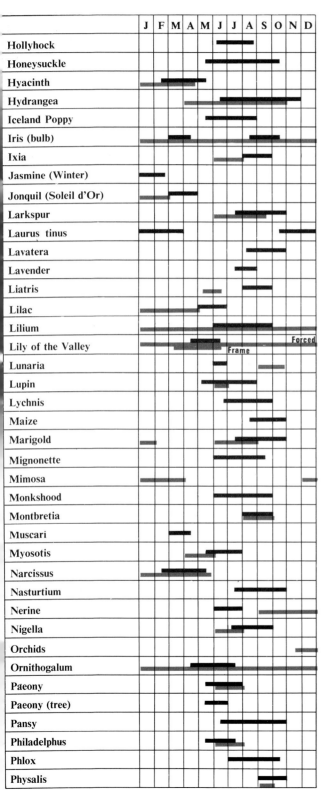

Left column plants: Hollyhock, Honeysuckle, Hyacinth, Hydrangea, Iceland Poppy, Iris (bulb), Ixia, Jasmine (Winter), Jonquil (Soleil d'Or), Larkspur, Laurus tinus, Lavatera, Lavender, Liatris, Lilac, Lilium, Lily of the Valley, Lunaria, Lupin, Lychnis, Maize, Marigold, Mignonette, Mimosa, Monkshood, Montbretia, Muscari, Myosotis, Narcissus, Nasturtium, Nerine, Nigella, Orchids, Ornithogalum, Paeony, Paeony (tree), Pansy, Philadelphus, Phlox, Physalis.

Right column plants: Pimento, Poinsettia, Polyanthus, Poppy, Primrose, Prunus triloba, Pyracantha (berry), Pyrethrum, Ranunculus, Rose, Rudbeckia, Scabious (annual), Scabious (perennial), Scilla, Snowdrop, Solidago, Spiraea, Statice, Stephanotis, Strelitzia, Sunflower, Sweet Peas, Sweet William, Symphoricarpos, Tamarix, Tritoma, Trollius, Tuberose, Tulip, Typha, Verbena, Violet, Water Lily, Wistaria, Yellow Stock, Zinnia.

139

INDEX

Back cover page _____

PRETORIA

A superb dried group suggesting a large candelabra with many arms, worked in dried and fresh flowers. A brilliant piece of floral art, suitable for a special buffet table. The candelabra is made from bases of pine cones and the whole arrangement set in a modern glass dish. The flowers are golden shower orchids and the Leucospermen or pin cushion Protea.

Editions Floraisse   -   All rights reserved **May 1975**   -   1st Edition   -   Legally Deposed No. 30   -   Printed in France